Gypsy Swing & Hot Club Rhythm
for Mandolin
by Dix Bruce

- Learn melodies & chord progressions to 12 great Gypsy Swing standards in the style recorded by Django Reinhardt, Stephane Grappelli, and the Quintette of the Hot Club of France

- Learn moveable closed position swing/jazz chords

- Learn the swing mandolin rhythm comp

- Jam along with a great "Hot Club"-style rhythm section

- Practice rhythm and soloing by playing along. ***We'll jam all night long!***

- Music includes standard notation, mandolin tablature, chords, & lyrics

P.O. Box 231005, Pleasant Hill, CA 94523
www.musixnow.com

902 BCD

Cover design by Charlotte Gibb. Back cover photo of Dix Bruce by Theresa Hioki.
Thanks to Brian Lambert, Sherry Shachter, and Brandt Williams for their most helpful suggestions.
Book and CD © Copyright 2007 by Dix Bruce

Contents

Introduction to Gypsy Swing 3

How to work with the book and CD 5

Swing Mandolin Rhythm 7

Avalon 8

The Sheik of Araby 10

Some of These Days 13

After You've Gone 16

Baby Won't You Please Come Home? 18

Swing in Minor 20

Chicago 23

China Boy 26

St. Louis Blues 28

Rose Room 32

Dark Eyes 34

Swingin' Like '42 37

CD Contents 40

Index 40

Introduction to Gypsy Swing

The music of the Quintette of the Hot Club of France with Django Reinhardt on guitar and Stephane Grappelli on violin is a kind of mystic holy grail for fans of string swing and jazz. Django and Stephane played with exceptional virtuosity, passion, excitement, and a life force that's still infectious over fifty years after they played their last notes together. The sound is, at times, unbelievable. How could human beings play with such precision and fire? And their music swings! When you hear it, you want to play along!

The purpose of this book and CD set is to get you started playing music in the Gypsy Swing and Hot Club style. You'll first learn "swing" chords and Hot Club-style rhythm playing on twelve great songs, most of which Django Reinhardt and Stephane Grappelli recorded. Then you can concentrate on the melodies and practice playing along with the recorded band. Finally, you'll develop your own solos and practice them with the band that never gets tired! In addition to having a lot of fun, you'll build a repertoire of songs, chords, chord progressions, melodies, and leads.

Start by reading the music in the book and playing along with the recorded rhythm sections, first at a slow speed with just guitar accompaniment, then, when you're ready, with a full blown "Hot Club"-style band. The band will play through each tune several times to give you the opportunity to practice rhythm chords and melodies and your own solo improvisations. It's just like having your own "Hot Club" band on call. You can work on a tune, solo, or passage for hours, perfecting it without wearing out your fellow players. The opportunities for advancing your reading and improvising skills while expanding your repertoire are unlimited. ***We'll jam all night long!***

All of the songs and chord progressions in the book and on the CD are essential, "must-know" pieces both in the Gypsy Swing world and in the larger world of Swing & Jazz. The music includes standard notation, tablature, chords, lyrics, chord diagrams, and suggested fingerings.

For the most part, the songs are presented in the keys the Hot Club played them in. There are exceptions and I took some liberties here and there for the sake of variety and harmonic interest. One of my goals with this project is to help make keys interchangeable to you and prepare you to play any song in any key with ease. Learning closed position chords and melodies will give you a great head start. You will snicker at songs written in five sharps, laugh out loud at four flats! Download my "Scale and Chord Chart" for reference. It shows all the major scales and chords for every key. It's a great tool for transposing. Go to the "Downloads" section of my web site: **www.musixnow.com**.

Measure numbers are shown beginning with the second staff of each song on the left hand side above the treble clef sign. I often refer to these numbers in the text accompanying the songs. Numbering starts after any pickup measures.

Melodies and rhythm section backups to all the tunes in this book are on the recording at slow and regular speeds. First you'll hear a melody played on mandolin slowly, with just guitar backup. Then you'll hear the same melody at regular speed, with the full band. Finally you'll hear the band playing the song from beginning to end, several times through, without any recorded lead. You'll play all the chords, melodies, solos and improvisations!

Most melodies are written with no open string notes. Likewise all chords are shown in closed position with no open strings. Beginning and intermediate mandolinists tend to perceive melodies or chords with open string notes as somehow easier than those with all closed position or fretted notes. That may be because melodies or chords with open string notes are more familiar than those with all closed position notes. However, there's a great advantage to knowing chords and melodies in closed positions. Closed position chords and entire chord progressions as well as melodies and solos can be easily moved up and down the fingerboard to new positions and keys. How might this come in handy? Suppose you learn "Avalon" as written in the key of F. Great, as long as the people you play with perform it in the same key. You might come across a tenor sax player who wants to perform the song in the key of Ab. If you know the chord progression or melody in a closed position, you simply move everything up three frets. The small numbers between the lyric and tablature lines are suggested fretting finger numbers for melodies. If you can't reach the notes with these fingers, feel free to change them. Chord diagrams include the same information and are explained further in the "Swing Rhythm Mandolin" section on page 7.

The recorded backup band plays in the style of the Quintette of the Hot Club of France and includes me, Dix Bruce, on rhythm mandolin and guitar; Jason Vanderford on rhythm guitar; and Steve Hanson on string bass. I also play the mandolin leads. Tuning tones are on track one of the CD. ***Let's get swingin'!***

l. to r.: Jason Vanderford, Steve Hanson, Dix Bruce.

Gypsy Swing & Hot Club Rhythm for Mandolin, Vol. II

More songs, *more* chords, *more* keys, *more* octaves, *more* swinging music in the **Gypsy Swing & Hot Club** style to learn and play. Widen your repertoire of Hot Club and Swing standards, chord forms, melodies and grooves. Same "jam along" format as this book/CD set with both regular and slow speeds plus extra projects and playing tips to explore. Log on to **www.musixnow** for info and updates. **We'll jam all night long!**

How to work with the book and CD

While it's true that there's not much history of mandolin in Gypsy Swing, there have been some great swing and jazz mandolinists, almost all of whom credit the music of the Quintette of the Hot Club of France as a major inspiration. Jethro Burns, Tiny Moore, and Dave Apollon come to mind immediately and David Grisman is probably the most important modern day advocate of the music. Of course mandolinists all over the world love and play this music with passion. I thought it was time to dedicate a book to the subject. My hope is that it will encourage and instruct a whole new generation of mandolinists in a few of the elements basic to a music that's close to my heart. One of you may become the Django Reinhardt or Stephane Grappelli of the mandolin!

- **Before you dive into a chord progression or melody, read along as you first listen to the recording.** It's a good idea to review the chords and scales of the key each song is in, especially if you are not used to playing in that key. Learn the chords and chord progressions by playing along with the slow version first. Gradually work your way up to the regular speed band version. If you're new to this style of music, there will be a lot to learn: chord positions, the rhythm comp, and the melody — not to mention any solos you develop or improvise.

- **When you've memorized the chords and the chord progression, try the melody**, again mastering the slow version before you move on to the full-speed band version. Then try moving the melody up or down an octave, according to what the instrument allows. Also try moving melodies to other keys. If the melody includes open string notes, find their fretted equivalents and transpose these melodies too.

- **Once you can play the melody along with the band, try making up your own solos.** Start by changing the memorized melodies slightly as you play along to make them "swing" more than the version on the printed page. By "rhythmizing" a given melody you can create an entirely new solo. I demonstrate this technique on several of the songs including "After You've Gone" on page 16 and "Chicago" on page 23. We'll work through transposing a melody up an octave on "The Sheik of Araby" on page 10. Apply these and the other exercises to all of the tunes in the book and play them again and again until you have something that feels like your own solo. Remember, the recorded band will back you up for hours with no complaints as you try this melody or that lick. It's a good idea to write out your improvisations and keep them in a spiral bound music notebook. That way you can refer back and revise them as you progress. Work with the slow recording of a song until you're ready for the full speed band version. You can isolate the lead part or rhythm from either version by simply adjusting the balance control on your stereo. If you're listening with headphones you can take one side off.

- **Listen to how musicians that you admire play these songs and how they solo on them.** The most obvious place to start is with the masters of Gypsy Swing: Django Reinhardt and Stephane Grappelli. Listen closely and try to analyze how they approach a melody or chord progression. Be encouraged to "borrow" from Django, Stephane, or other masters. Learn their vocabularies and how they assemble phrases into a coherent whole. Learning to improvise in music is a lot like learning to speak. We all have the same letters, words and phrases which we continually recycle into sentences and paragraphs that, hopefully, express what we're feeling. The goal is to build your own musical/swing vocabulary which will eventually allow you to speak through your instrument.

- **As you're listening for inspiration, don't limit yourself to mandolin or guitar players.** Listen to everybody that you think is great, no matter what instrument they play. Stephane Grappelli is a great inspiration for playing in the Gypsy Swing style. Much of what he plays on the violin will work beautifully on mandolin. Identify what it is about a musician's playing or singing that moves you. Try to incorporate some of that in your own playing. Make yourself curious enough to listen to your favorite recorded musicians play a lick or passage until you figure it out — a hundred times if necessary.

- **Experiment with leaving the melodies completely behind you.** Sing along with the tracks and vocalize your ideas. Learn to sing what you're trying to play, even if you think you have a lousy voice. Look for new ideas and input constantly, and try to make them a part of your playing. Practice playing whatever is in your mind and heart. Don't quit working with the track after one solo — especially if it doesn't sound as good as you want right away — work it through the whole track. One of the advantages of the back up track is that you can try out an idea and play it on several solos in succession gaining control of it as you go.

• **Make the recorded band *your* band and work out with it daily.** The more you play, the better you'll play. You'll gain strength, stamina, and focus as you train yourself to play two, three, four or more solos in a row. A typical gig might consist of four one-hour sets with fifteen minute breaks in between. Start by jamming along with the CD for ten to fifteen minutes a day and work up from there. Check out my other "play along with the band" book and CD sets: **Gypsy Swing & Hot Club Rhythm, Vol. II for Mandolin, BackUP TRAX: Swing & Jazz** (includes mandolin TAB), **BackUP TRAX: Early Jazz & Hot Tunes,** and **BackUP TRAX: Traditional Jazz & Dixieland**. Though **Early Jazz** and **Traditional Jazz** don't include mandolin TAB, you'll still enjoy jamming along. Same with **BackUP TRAX: Basic Blues** (includes guitar TAB). Full details and audio samples are available on my web site: **www.musixnow.com**. If you play enough you'll eventually find that ideas and solos will begin to emerge. It's an incredibly rewarding process of discovery!

Michael Dregni wrote a great biography of Django Reinhardt titled "Django: The Life and Times of a Gypsy Legend" (Oxford University Press). For more information on Stephane Grappelli, you'll love the 2-DVD release "A Life in the Jazz Century" (Music on Earth). It includes all known film footage of Django Reinhardt.

If you're interested in transcriptions of Django's recorded solos see "The Music of Django Reinhardt: Forty Four Classic Solos by the Legandary Guitarist with Complete Analysis" by Stan Ayeroff. It includes transcriptions of Django solos on most of the tunes in this book. For transcriptions with guitar tablature of Django's original compositions, including "Swing 42," "Minor Swing," "Nuages," and many more, see "Complete Django: The Ultimate Django Book" by Max Robin and Jean-Phillipe Watremez. The first is available through my website: **www.musixnow.com**. Many of Stephane Grappelli's recorded solos are transcribed in Matt Glazer's "Jazz Violin." Violinists will enjoy a book/2CD set by Jeremy Cohen and I titled "Swing Jazz Violin with Hot Club Rhythm." (String Letter Publishing) It includes all twelve of the songs from this book arranged for violin, plus four additional titles and two jazz string quartet arrangements. Jeremy also wrote and recorded solos to all the songs and included informative instruction on playing violin in the jazz and Gypsy Swing style. It's available from my website: **www.musixnow.com**.

There are countless reissues of the music of the Quintette of the Hot Club of France and of Django and Stephane's recordings. Some of the best and most economical are the four and five disc sets on JSP Records. I recommend "Django Reinhardt: The Classic Early Recordings in Chronological Order" (JSPCD901), "Django Reinhardt Vol. 2: Paris and London 1937 to 1948" (JSPCD904), and "Django in Rome 1949/1950" (JSP919). Stephane Grappelli is included in all three sets. The first consists mainly of classic Hot Club material and in order to understand the music in this book, you *must* hear it. "Django in Rome 1949/1950" is interesting in that it presents Django and Stephane with a more "modern," non-Hot Club style rhythm section with piano, bass, and drums. It's all great music!

Now let's jam!

Dix Bruce (June 2007)

Dix Bruce is a writer and award-winning musician from the San Francisco Bay Area. He edited **Mandolin World News** *from 1978 to 1984. He has produced over fifty instructional book/CD sets and videos, most for Mel Bay Publications. His most recent DVD is "Swing & Jazz Mandolin: Chords & Rhythm." Dix has played guitar with San Francisco's Royal Society Jazz Orchestra since the late 1980s. Visit him online at www.musixnow.com.*

Swing Mandolin Rhythm

Swing mandolin rhythm is a combination of two elements:

- closed position moveable chords, and
- the "comp" or pulse of the strummed closed position chords.

In many styles of music, chords are strummed and the notes are allowed to ring. In swing and jazz we use closed position chords with no open string notes because we want to be able to control how long the notes of the chord ring to set up our rhythmic groove. We also want these chords to be moveable to other positions and keys. The familiar G7 below left has open string notes. If we strum the chord, strings three and four (string one is the thinest and shown on the right in chord diagrams, string four the fattest and shown on the left in chord diagrams) will continue to ring even if we lift our first and second fingers after we strum it. The G7 on the right below is a closed position form. The "x" under string one of the chord diagram tells us to mute or not play that string. (The open first string E note is not part of the G7 chord.) In this closed G7 form the side of my first finger mutes the first string. The "r" under string four of the G7 at left shows where the root (G in this G7 chord) is located if it's present in the form. Many of the chord forms we'll use won't include a root. Muting the chord while strumming is accomplished by loosening the fretting hand grip just enough after the strum to stop the sound. The number to the right of some of the chord diagrams tells us at which fret to place the form.

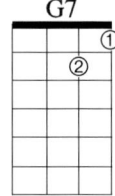 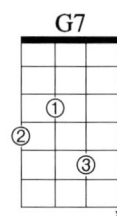

Chord diagrams are shown with the individual songs in the approximate order they appear in a progression. In some cases alternate fingerings or forms are also given. Try them all and see how each works in a particular situation. One might sound better or be easier to move in and out of than another. Try substituting other versions of the same chord from other songs in the book. Each form has a slightly different tonal color but an A7 is an A7 is an A7. Remember: for the sake of the rhythmic comp, use closed chord forms with no open string notes. Remember to swap out chords of the same quality: an A7 for an A7, an Am6 for an Am6, but not an A7 for an Am6.

The "comp" is a pattern of strumming with the picking hand and pulsing with the fretting hand to set up a groove that propels the rhythm. Let's look at 4/4 rhythm, which is the most prevalent meter in Swing and Gypsy Swing. In 4/4 we play four beats to the measure: 1 — 2 — 3 — 4. To play the comp we let strums one and three ring a bit but mute two and four after they're played. That gives the kind of "cha — chuk — cha — chuk" rhythm that Django and Stephane usually had behind them in the Quintette. According to Michael Dregni, the author of "Django: The Life and Times of a Gypsy Legend," this rhythm became known as *la pompe* or "the pump." Dregni describes it as: "striking each beat with a percussive strum, any sustain choked off by dampening the strings immediately after the downward strum." Listen to the demonstration of the comp in 4/4 and 3/4 on track two of the CD. As you listen to the full rhythm tracks, notice the difference in the way Jason Vanderford and I approach the comp. Jason's is very percussive, like Dregni describes above, almost like a snare drum, without much harmonic content. I let my strums ring a little longer and you hear the notes of the chord a bit more. I think the two styles work well together and I very much enjoyed playing with both Jason and Steve Hanson.

The mandolin I play on the recordings was built by Bob Schneider. It's a wonderful instrument, a kind of modified oval soundhole F4 of Bob's own design. It's got an incredibly rich, reverberant tone. It's pictured on the cover of this book. The Schneider website is: www.schneiderF5.com.

Avalon

"Avalon" is a popular standard from 1920. The composers are listed in the original sheet music as Al Jolson and Vincent Rose. I've always wondered if Jolson actually had a hand in composing the song or if he bought into it, which was common practice for big stars of the time.

The melody is made up primarily of half notes and played at a quick tempo. The effect is to make the accompaniment sound as if it's in double time. The four measure string bass introduction is similar to one on a recording of "Avalon" by Django Reinhardt and Stephane Grappelli with the Quintette of the Hot Club of France. Occasionally an introduction is added to a song form. In this case, the string bass plays the riff unaccompanied, one time, at the very beginning of the tune. You, as a member of the band, need to be able to recognize where the intro ends and where the form of the song begins.

Try substituting the F6 for the F chords in the progression, especially for the F in the last two measures.

The ending we recorded is a common and fun Hot Club / traditional jazz-style ending. The band stops after an accented break on beat one of the F (or "one") chord of measure thirty one of the last chorus. After that I continue by sliding a tremoloed chord form up the guitar fingerboard from C to F to end on a last hit with the band. Try the same thing on mandolin.

I added some substitute chords in parenthesis in measures nine through twelve. When a chord progression stays on a five dominant (V) chord, in this case a C7, for several measures, we can often swap in a two minor seven chord (ii m7), a Gm7 here. Try this alternate progression and see if you like it. You could also plug these changes in at measures one through four. Identify other extended passages of dominant seven chords in this and other songs and experiment with adding in the appropriate ii and m7 chords.

By the way, the lyrics to all the songs are included. Even if you're not a singer, I think it's important to know a song by its lyrics. I often have them running in my head as I play a melody or compose a solo. It helps me stay grounded on each specific song.

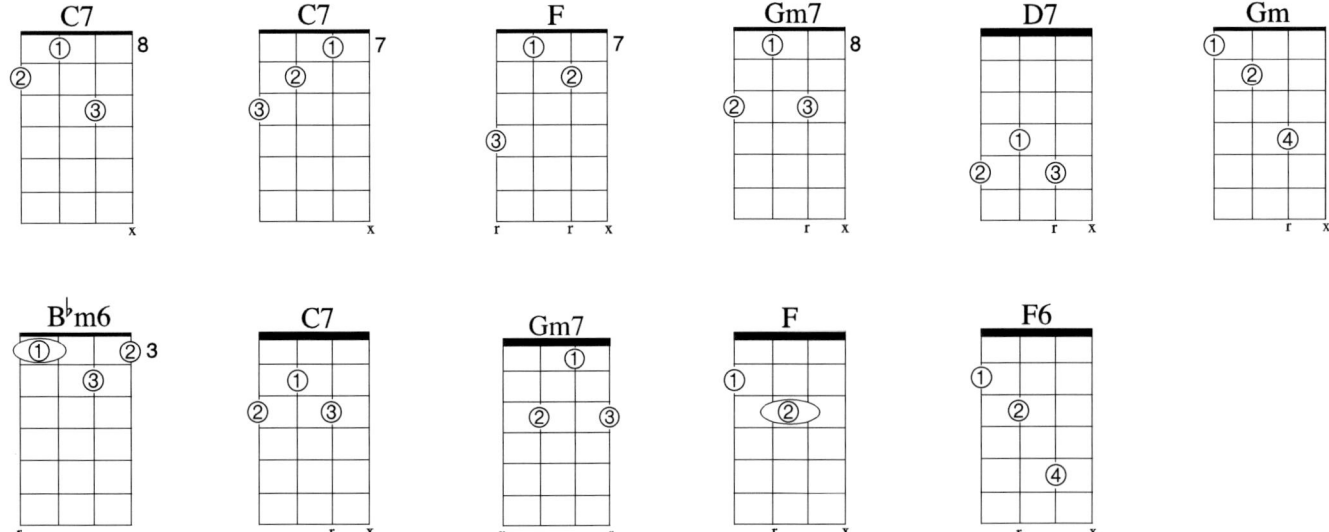

Avalon

Key of F, CD tracks 3-5

Jolson & Rose, 1920

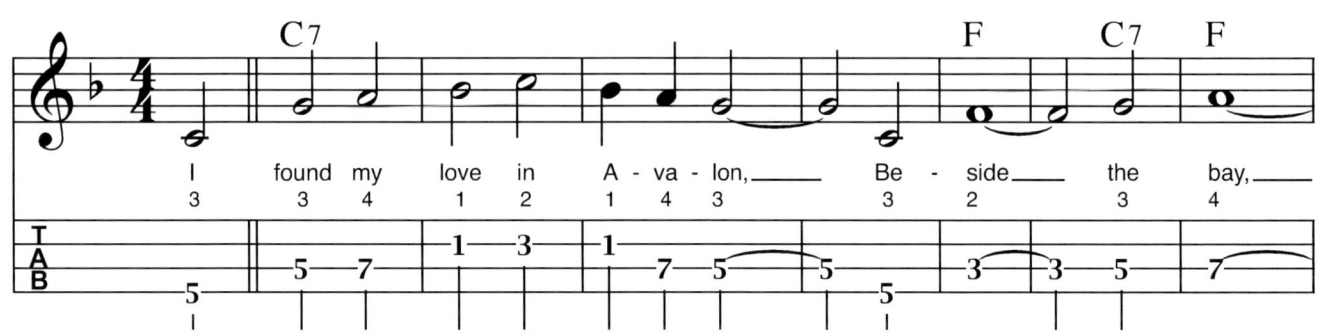
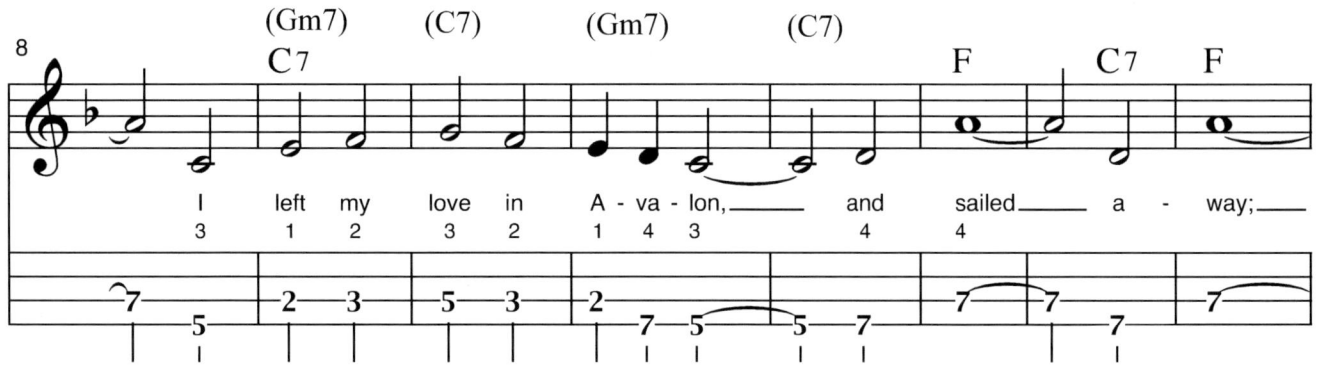

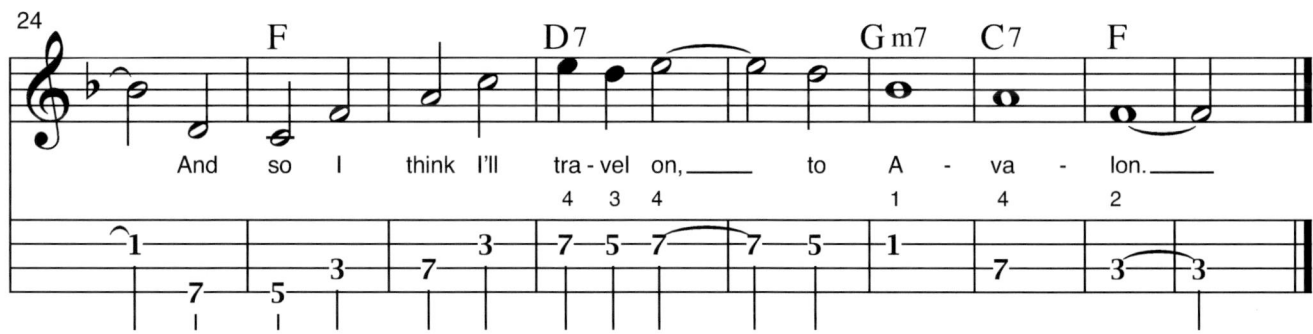

Arrangement © 2007 by Dix Bruce

The Sheik of Araby

"The Sheik of Araby" first appeared in 1921 and has been a popular standard ever since. It's usually played in the key of Bb, which is where I've written it below. The melody is a combination of staccato and legato notes with a repetitive rhythmic motif: quarter notes followed by dotted halves.

As mentioned in the introduction, most of the melodies in this book are written in closed position with no open string notes. The great advantage of learning a melody or solo in a closed position is that you can easily move it up or down the fingerboard to different keys. For example, once you have the chord progression or melody to "The Sheik" memorized, move it up two frets and you'll be in the key of C. In "The Sheik of Araby" you'll find several seventh fret third string A notes (measures eight, nine, fourteen, twenty eight and twenty nine) played with the fourth finger. You *could* play these A notes on the open second string but then you wouldn't have a closed position moveable melody.

Because the mandolin is tuned in fifths, that is, the interval between any two adjacent strings is a perfect fifth, melodies can also be moved *across* as well as up and down the fingerboard. This gives you another way to transpose a melody to a different key. When you've memorized the first, lower octave version of "The Sheik" on page 11, try moving it "over" one string so that your first note is on the third fret of string four. Keep the relative positions of the other notes in tact and you'll move the melody to the key of Eb. After that, try the upper octave version on page 12. In this example we'll stay in the key of Bb and move the melody up a full octave. As you'll see, your fingerings will be exactly the same as in the lower octave version though on different strings. Be sure to try these types of modulation on every melody. If a melody has open string notes, move them to a fretted position.

For the longer, sustained notes in "The Sheik" and other songs in this set, I used tremolo, especially on the slower versions. Without it, the notes decay quite quickly. I like the extra sustain that tremolo allows. The difficulty can be in getting the tremolo started and controlling it to end where you want it to end cleanly. It's good to practice starting and stopping your tremolo. Whether you use tremolo or not is ultimately an artistic decision. You could just as easily play "The Sheik" without any tremolo at all or only on selected notes.

The ending is one of those "chord tremolo windup, take no prisoners, the song is over, now go home" type of things. Remember: it's always nice when the band ends together!

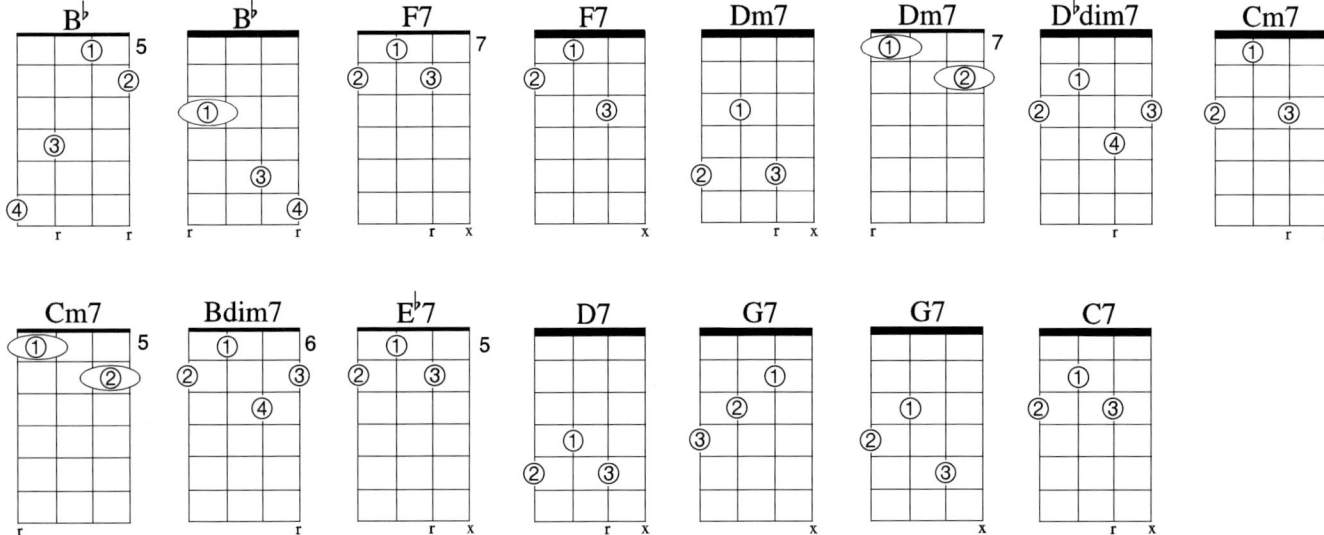

The Sheik of Araby

Key of Bb, CD tracks 6-8
T. Snyder, H. Smith, & F. Wheeler, 1921

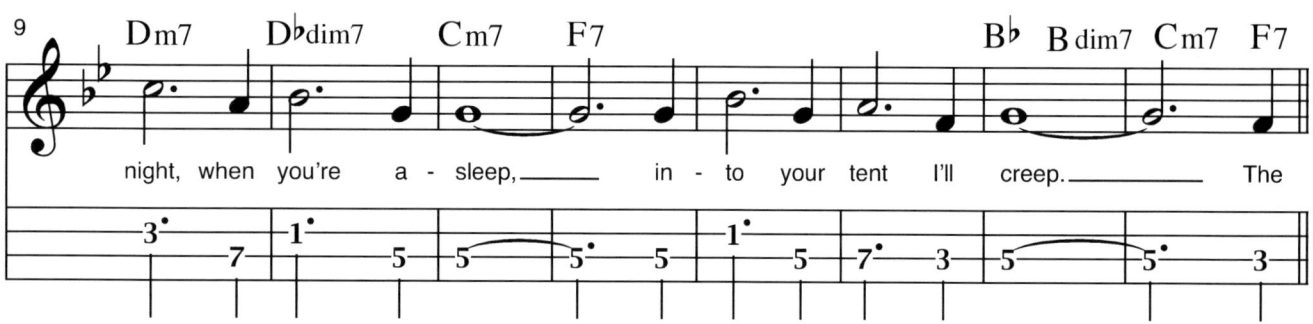

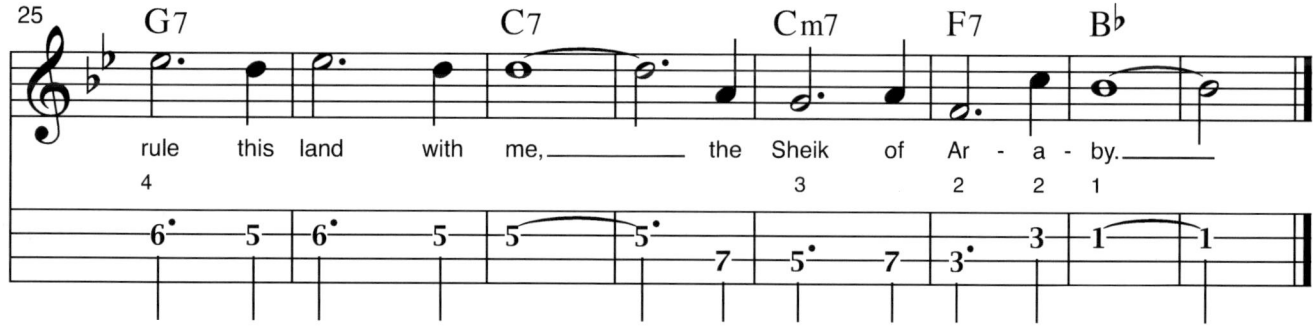

Arrangement © 2007 by Dix Bruce • www.musixnow.com

The Sheik of Araby transposed up an octave:

Arrangement © 2007 by Dix Bruce • www.musixnow.com

Some of These Days

"Some of These Days" is a favorite of Red Hot Mama singers the world over. One of its interesting aspects is that it modulates between the keys of E minor and G major. E minor is the relative minor of G; G is the relative major of E minor and they share the same scale and key signature.

I diverge a bit here and there from the straight rhythm and add accents and counter rhythms on guitar. Django would often add little rhythmic flourishes like these behind Stephane's solos. As with everything he played, Django was a master of these rhythmic accents. When I add rhythmic variations I try to keep them to a minimum so they won't detract from the groove or compete with what the soloist is playing. There's always a danger of adding too much. Accents like these could be played on mandolin as well as guitar.

I've listed alternate voicings for some of the chords below, notably the B7 and Em. As I mentioned before, any B7 will technically work for any other B7. You'll decide which to use by its sound or how it fits with the chords preceding and following. Try to compile sets of chords that don't require big jumps on the fingerboard. Many of these changes require that you move only one note to go from chord to chord. Explore these tight voicings and practice sets of changes that need only minimal fretting hand shifts. Feel free to bring in your own chord voicings or voicings from other songs in the book. The bottom line will always be sound and you may decide to use forms that require wide hand movements.

The melody has a lot of chromatic tones in it as you can see from all the accidentals (sharps and flats). As a result, the suggested fingerings shift around a bit and you won't always play the same note at the same fret with the same finger. If you find the given fretting finger suggestions difficult, experiment with your own positions and fingerings.

After you can play the melody as written, move all the open second string A notes to the third string seventh fret. Move the open first string E notes to the second string seventh fret. It'll be good for you, I promise!

I took liberties with the melody, especially on the up-to-speed recording. I tried to "swingify" it a bit by adding a few more notes, somes slides, and some rhythmic stretches. I wanted it to be more alive and intense than a strict reading of the written melody would be. Is this legal? You bet it is! Not only are we jazz musicians, we are mandolinic jazz musicians. We're supposed to do this!

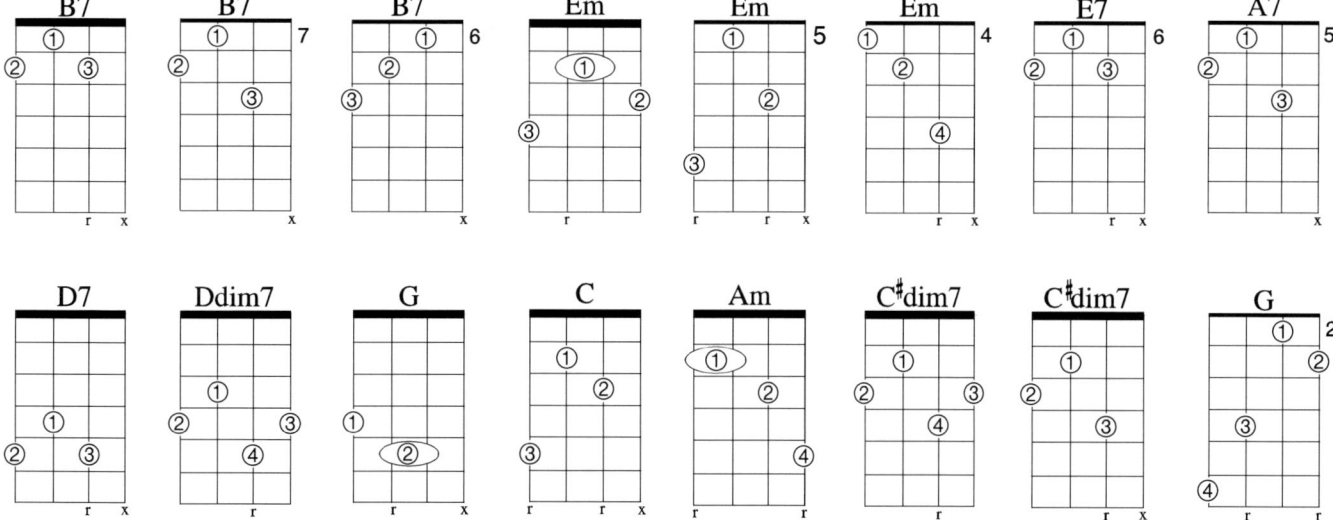

Some of These Days

Key of Em, G, CD tracks 9-11
Sheldon Brooks, 1910

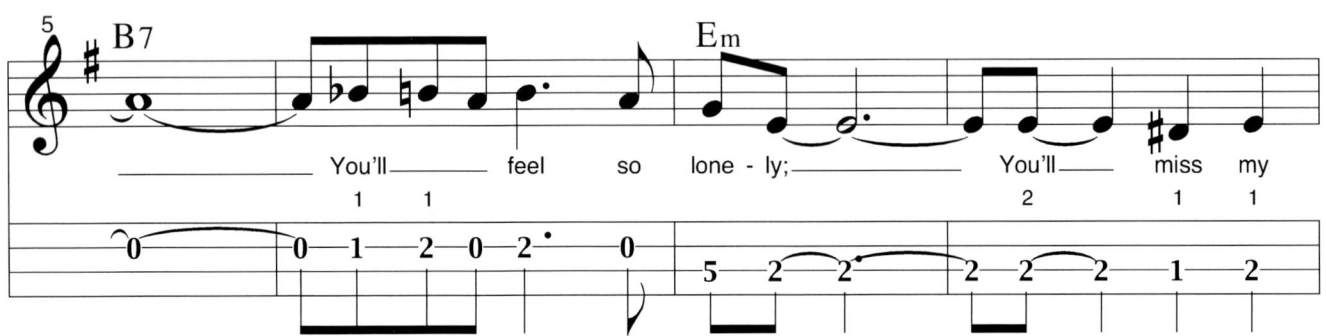
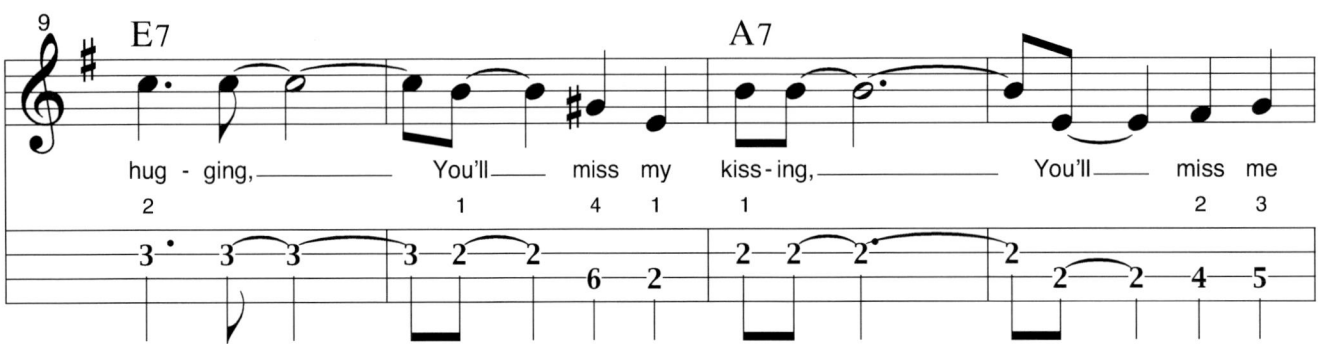
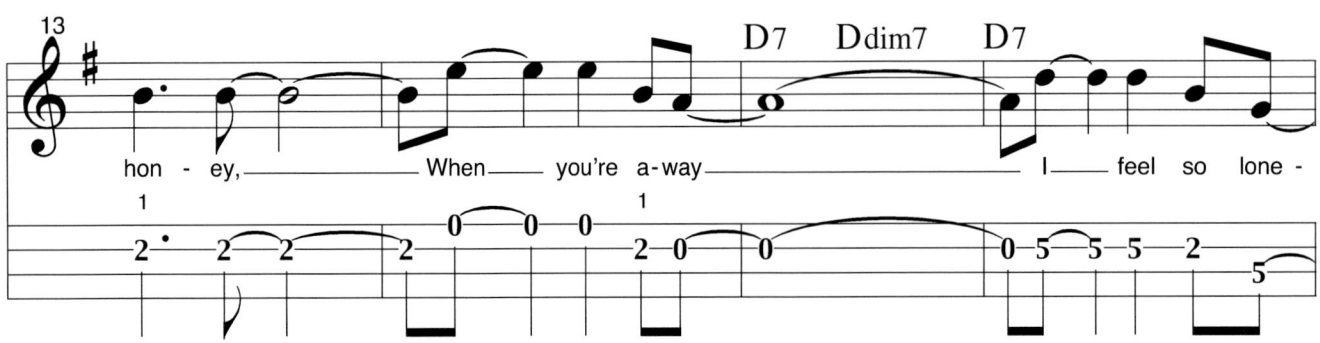

Arrangement © 2007 by Dix Bruce • www.musixnow.com

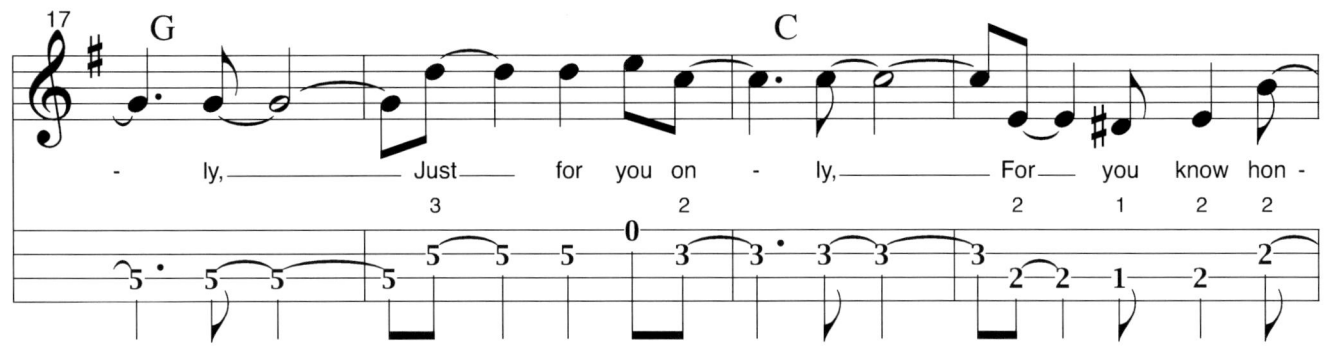
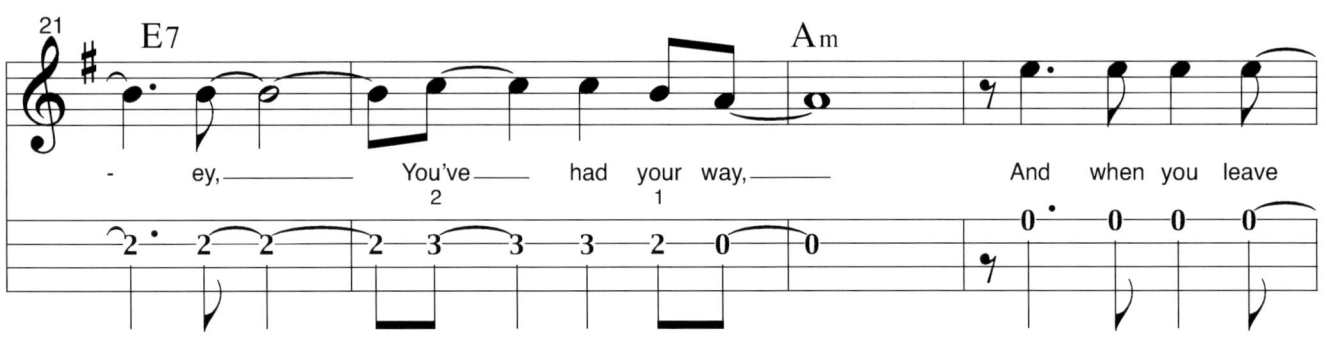

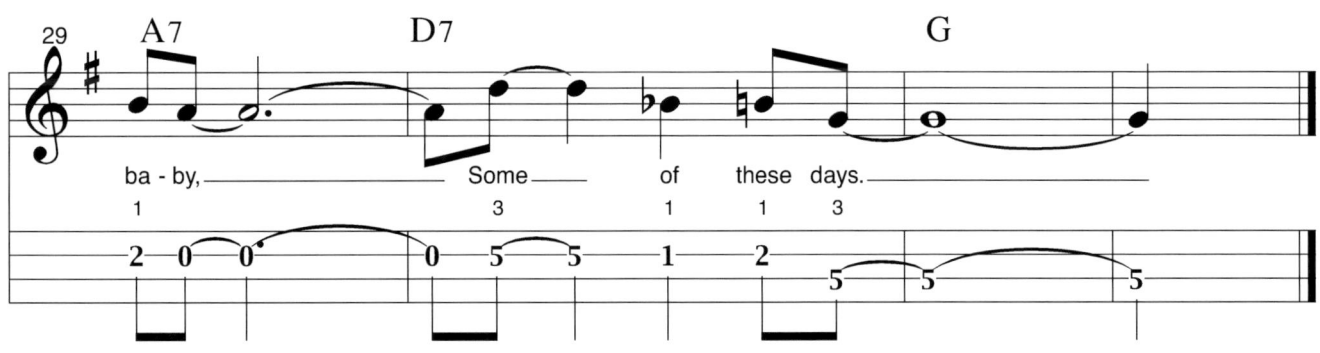

After You've Gone

"After You've Gone" is another great standard played by jazz musicians *everywhere*! It's a bit unusual in that the first chord of measure one is a IV ("four chord") in this case an F. That might lead you to conclude that the song is in the key of F when it's actually in the key of C. The foolproof way to know what key a piece is in is to look at the key signature, the space between the treble clef sign and time signature on the left hand side of the music. The number of sharps or flats will define the key.

The example above from "Avalon" has one flat in its key signature and that means that the song is in the key of F, even though the first chord is a C7. If there are no sharps or flats in the key signature, which is the case with "After You've Gone," the piece is in the key of C. For more info on the numbers of sharps and flats in keys, download the "Scale and Chord Chart" from **www.musixnow.com.** Another fairly reliable method for determining the key of a piece is to find what chord the song ends on. If it ends on a C chord, the piece is probably in the key of C. If it ends on a Bb chord, then it's most likely in the key of Bb. If it ends on a Dm chord, the piece is probably in D minor. There are exceptions, but they're rare in pop and jazz.

As with "Some of These Days," I didn't play the up-to-speed melody exactly as written but added a few slides and rhythmic syncopations here and there when I recorded it. This is typical of a jazz interpretation of a melody. You can use this type of interpretation to compose melody-based solos.

We played a stop or "break" in the rhythm track at measure thirteen on the last time through. I kept a rhythm click going on the guitar to guide you. Having a break like this is a very common tool that musicians use to add interest and tension to a performance. As a player you need to be able to count the rhythm in your head and not loose the groove. This break will give you practice counting.

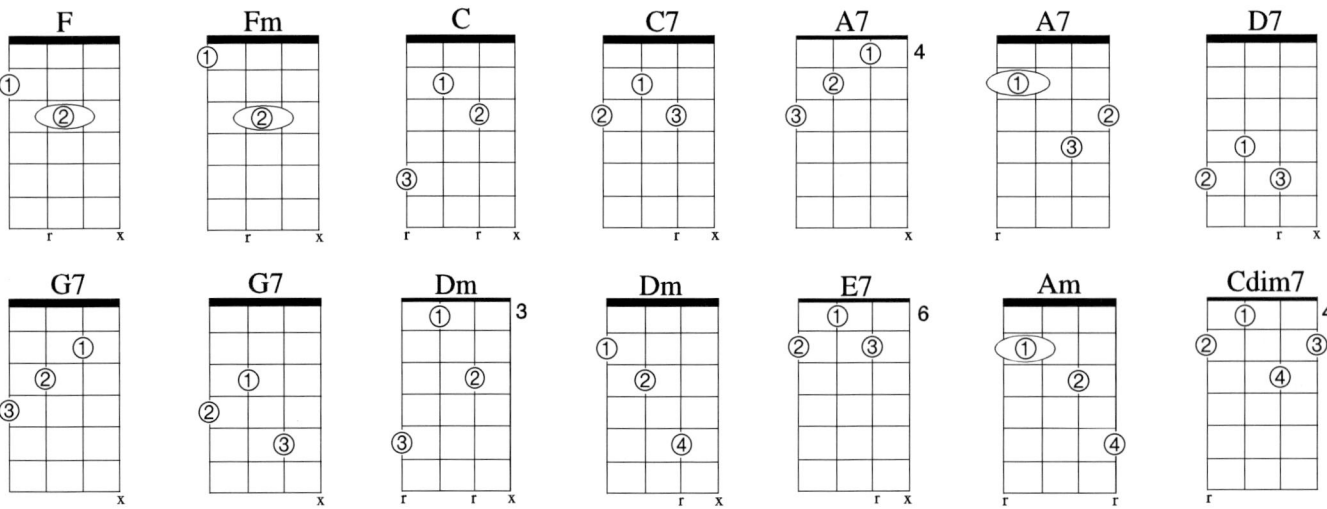

16 Gypsy Swing & Hot Club Rhythm for Mandolin

After You've Gone

Key of C, CD tracks 12-14 — Creamer & Layton, 1918

Baby Won't You Please Come Home?

"Baby Won't You Please Come Home?" is in the key of Eb. If you're not used to it, playing in flat keys like Eb, Bb, Ab, etc., can strike fear into your heart. Once you've had experience playing in different keys, you'll find that one key is pretty much the same as any other. If you want to play swing and jazz, it's important that you reach that point. Different players and especially different singers, will want to perform songs in different keys. For example, a horn player might like flat keys like F, Bb, Eb, etc., or a singer may need to move "Baby Won't You Please Come Home" from Eb to the key of C or G. Since the singer can't adjust his or her range, you need to adjust what you play to where they need to sing. Be prepared! Don't shy away from keys and sets of chords that you might find initially challenging. Practice moving all the songs in this book to a variety of other keys. The "Scale and Chord Chart" that you can download from www.musixnow.com will show you how to transpose the chords to any key.

The tablature to "Baby Won't You Please Come Home?" includes some open string notes. After you can play the melody as written, try moving the open string notes to closed, fretted positions.

"Baby Won't You Please Come Home" has an unusual form: it's eighteen measures in length. Most of the other songs in this book and in the jazz / pop repertoire are built on sixteen or thirty two bar forms. "Baby Won't You Please Come Home" has two additional bars that include a built in "I really mean it!" Here's where the singer drops to one knee and really "sells" the song.

The last two measures of the last chorus of the rhythm track are extended. Instead of playing two beats each of the F7 and Bb7 chords, we play four beats or one whole measure of each. There are several types of extended and special endings like this in Gypsy Swing and Jazz and we'll explore a few of them in this book.

Below you'll see additional forms of the G7, Bb7, Cm, and Ab chords. The different forms are interchangeable though each has a unique sound. Try using the form that's closest to the chords that occur before and after to avoid an awkward hand shift.

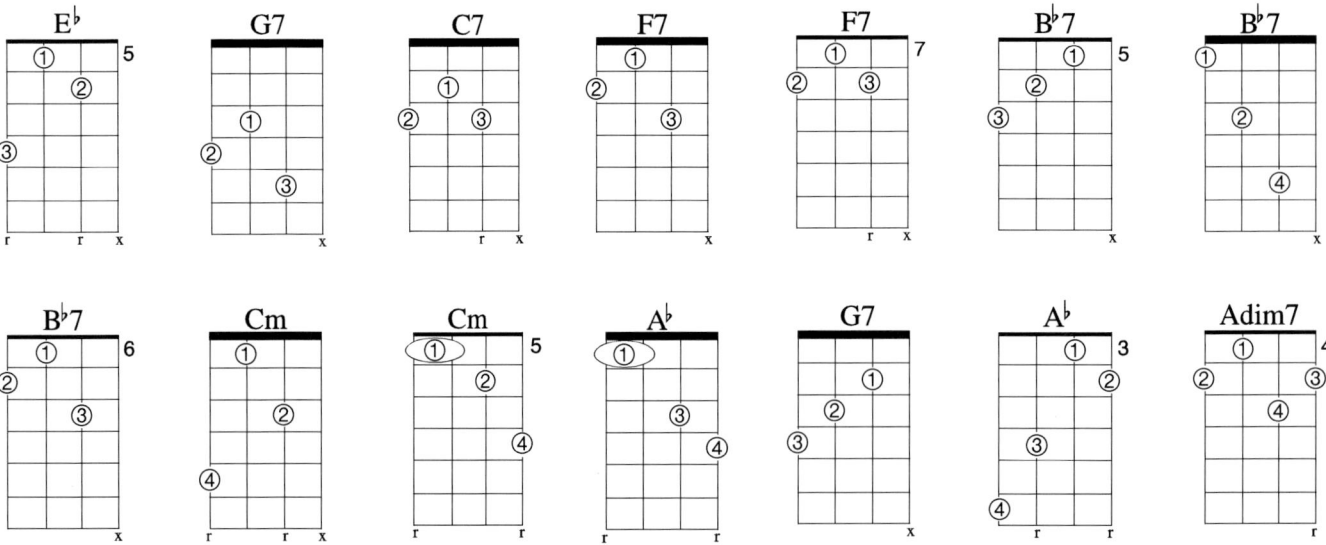

Baby Won't You Please Come Home?

Key of Eb, CD tracks 15-17   C. Williams & C. Warfield, 1919

Arrangement © 2007 by Dix Bruce • www.musixnow.com

Swing in Minor

"Swing in Minor" is based on a famous Django Reinhardt and Stephane Grappelli composition called "Minor Swing." Django and Stephane recorded it several times and played it in the key of Am, so that's where "Swing in Minor" is set. David Grisman recorded a wonderful arrangement of "Minor Swing" in the late 1970s in the key of Dm. Grisman's version is well-known among acoustic string players. Check out the Dm version of "Swing in Minor" on page 22. Unfortunately we didn't have room for a track in Dm on the CD. You can use the melody to "Swing in Minor" in either key as a solo over the changes to "Minor Swing."

"Swing in Minor" has a somewhat unusual form with two different melodies or "heads." One is played at the beginning of the tune, one at the end. We've edited the two together on the CD so you can practice both. As you'll hear, both are punctuated by band breaks or stops with fills by the string bass. Since the band plays one whole note in every measure in the first part it is incumbent on the soloist to provide very clear swing rhythm structure and timing.

The harmonics played at the end of the up-to-speed melody are played at the twelfth fret on strings one and two. To play a harmonic lay a fretting finger lightly on the string pair over the fret wire, in this case the twelfth. Don't press down but pick the string as usual. Work toward getting a chime-like sound.

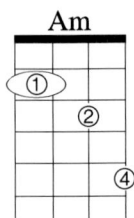 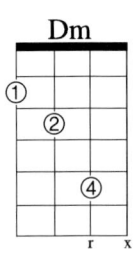 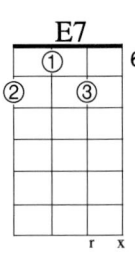 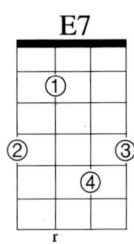 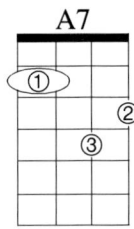 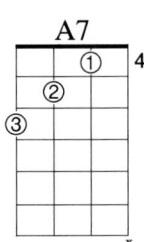 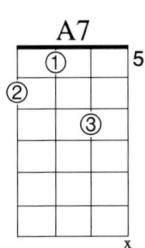

Chords for the key of Dm version on page 22:

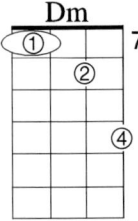 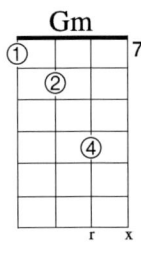 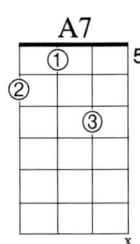 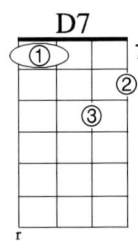 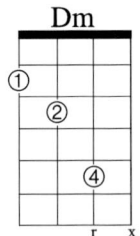 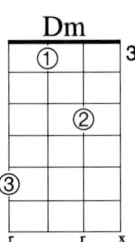

Swing in Minor

Key of Am, CD tracks 18-20
Dix Bruce, 2007

Swing in Minor moved to Dm

Copyright © 2007 by Dix Bruce • Dix Bruce Music (BMI) • www.musixnow.com

Chicago

"Chicago" has been a jazz standard since it was introduced in the early 1920s. It was written by the great Fred Fisher, who also wrote "Peg o' My Heart," "Dardanella," "Daddy, You've Been a Mother to Me," and "Your Feet's Too Big." "Chicago" has a slightly unusual form where only the first four measures are repeated. The melody is built around a repetitive syncopated rhythmic riff. You'll hear it again and again with the lyrics "Chi-ca-go, Chi-ca-go." As you work through the melody, try to get that same swing and bounce. You'll notice that I significantly "swingified" the fast version of the melody. The rhythm just seemed to demand it!

Lots and lots of chords in the accompaniment department! They're all great forms that you'll use again and again in this style of music. In some cases I gave you more than one form to choose from.

We added a break in the rhythm after the first chorus. Jason plays a rhythm click during the break to keep the band honest, rhythm-wise. In a real life band situation, probably only the soloist would be playing here. You need to keep the rhythm in your head and come in at the right time at the top of the next chorus.

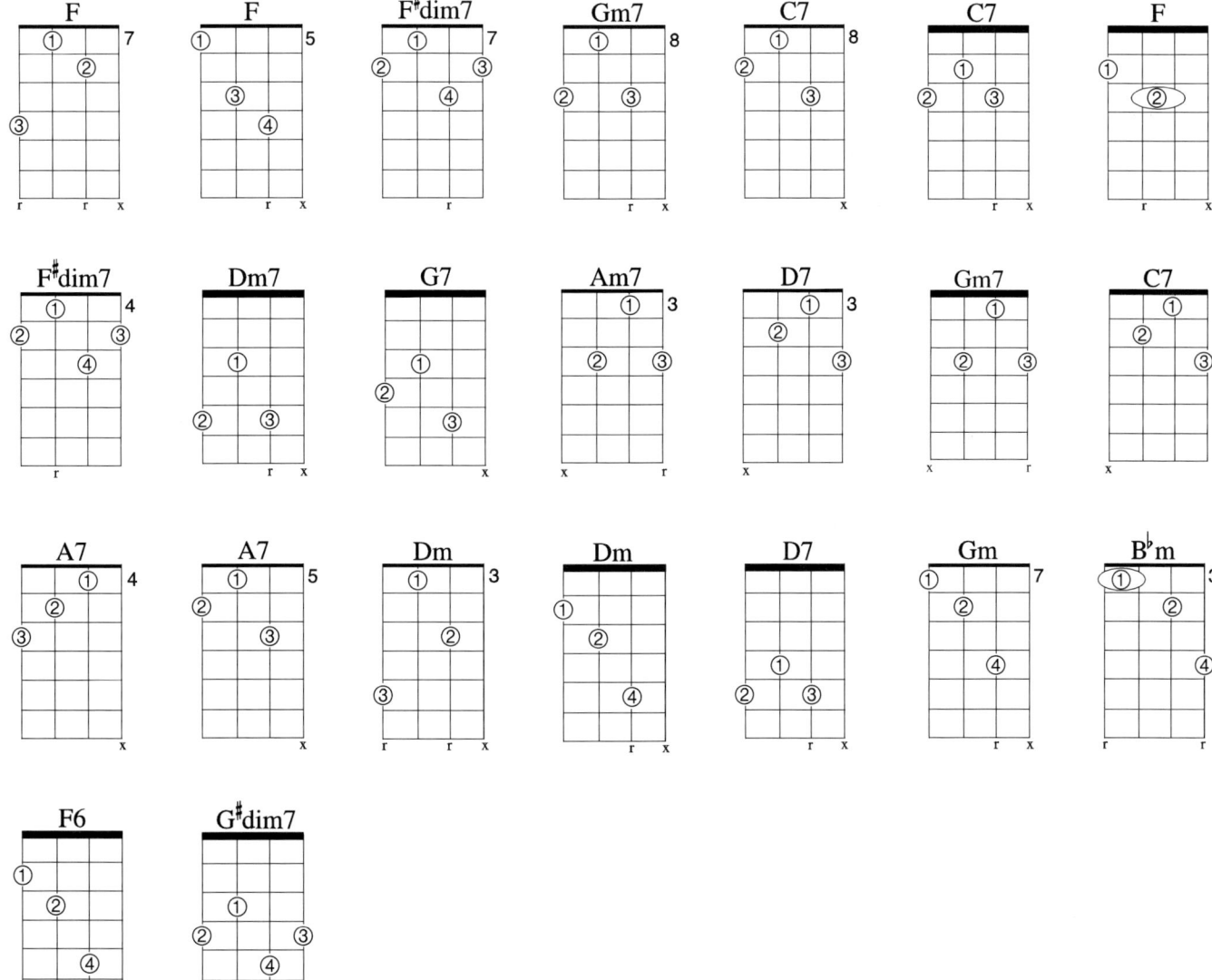

Gypsy Swing & Hot Club Rhythm for Mandolin

Chicago

Key of F, CD tracks 21-23
F. Fisher, 1922

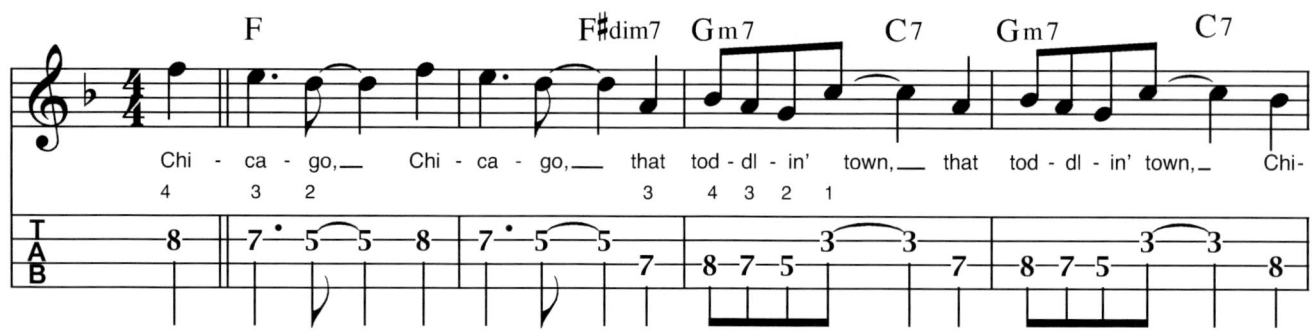
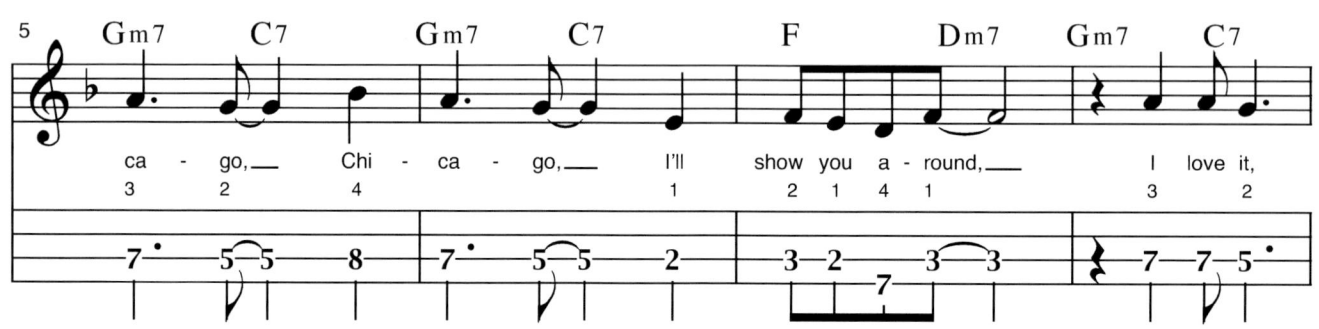
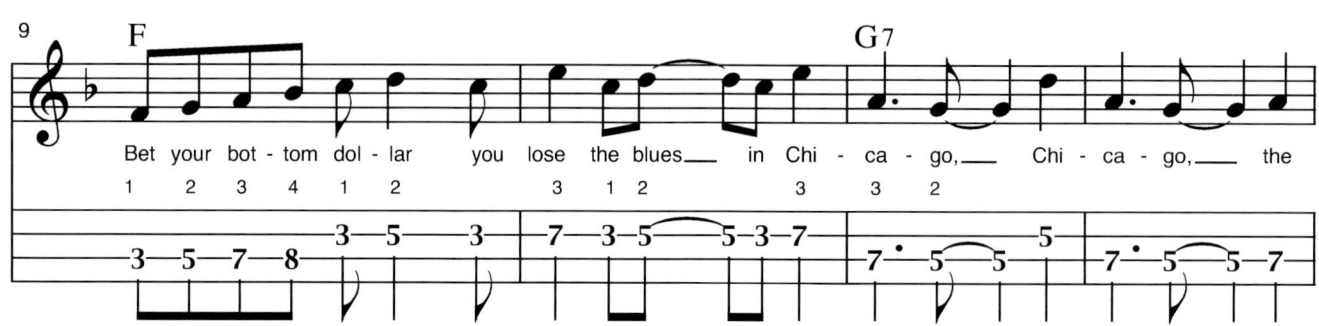

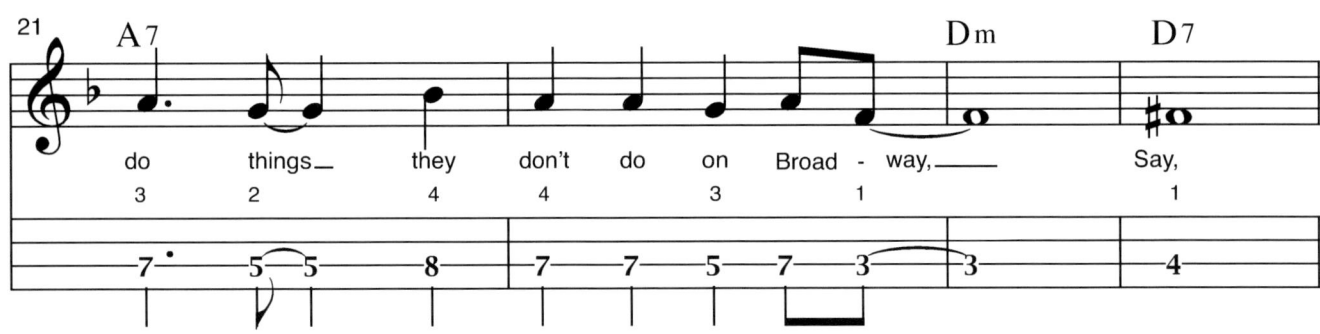

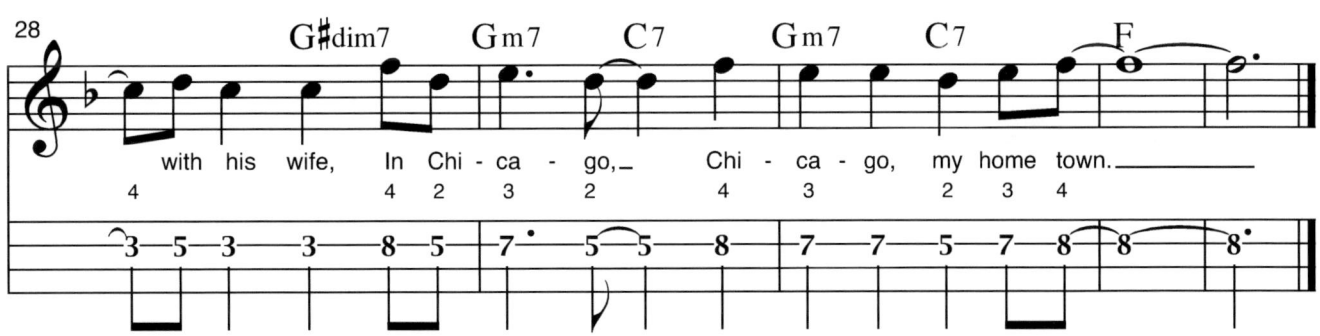

China Boy

"China Boy" has a relatively simple and straight forward legato melody with lots of long, flowing, smooth notes. It starts out in the key of F but modulates to the key of Ab in measure sixteen with the Eb7 chord. The song stays in Ab until measure twenty four where the C7 chord, the V chord of the original key of F, moves it back to the key of F. The modulations give the song an interesting ebb and flow. They also necessitate two quite different fretting hand positions which are reflected in the tablature and fretting hand finger suggestions.

On the track I play the melody very close to the way it's written with some syncopations and anticipations to swing it up a bit. Remember: you don't want to play these melodies exactly as written. Be sure to add your own swing and jazz phrasing. If you're not sure what this means, spend some time listening to Django and Stephane and compare what they do to the written versions of these songs.

The melody to "China Boy" has no open string notes, they're all fretted and located on strings two and three. That makes it a great candidate to move "over" one string and transpose the melody to a new key. Try playing your first note on the seventh fret of string four. Keep the relative note positions the same and play them on strings three and four instead of strings two and three. (You'll play the same TAB numbers on different strings and be in the key of Bb.) Once you can do that, try playing your first note on the seventh fret of string two. All your notes will be on strings one and two and you will have transposed "China Boy" to the key of C. Again, play the same relative note positions. Ain't that the coolest thing? You can also move any of these positions *up* the fingerboard. For example, start the original melody on string three, fret nine to transpose the melody to the key of G.

The slow version of the melody on the CD has no tremolo, the up-to-speed melody does. Try it both ways and see which you prefer.

At about 2:04 into the band track I do a little extra rhythm riff on the guitar. You can do things like this when you have a second player holding down the rhythm like Jason Vanderford does. I picked a riff that fit with what Jason and Steve Hanson were playing and worked it again and again through the changes and up to the modulation where I reverted to regular rhythm. Then I went back to the rhythm riff for the last eight measures of the key of F part. I do a similar rhythm riff on mandolin in the last chorus, which begins about 3:00. The ending to the track has another typical Django-esque windup and abrupt ending. They're fun to do, they wake up the audience and the band and leave no doubt as to where the song ends.

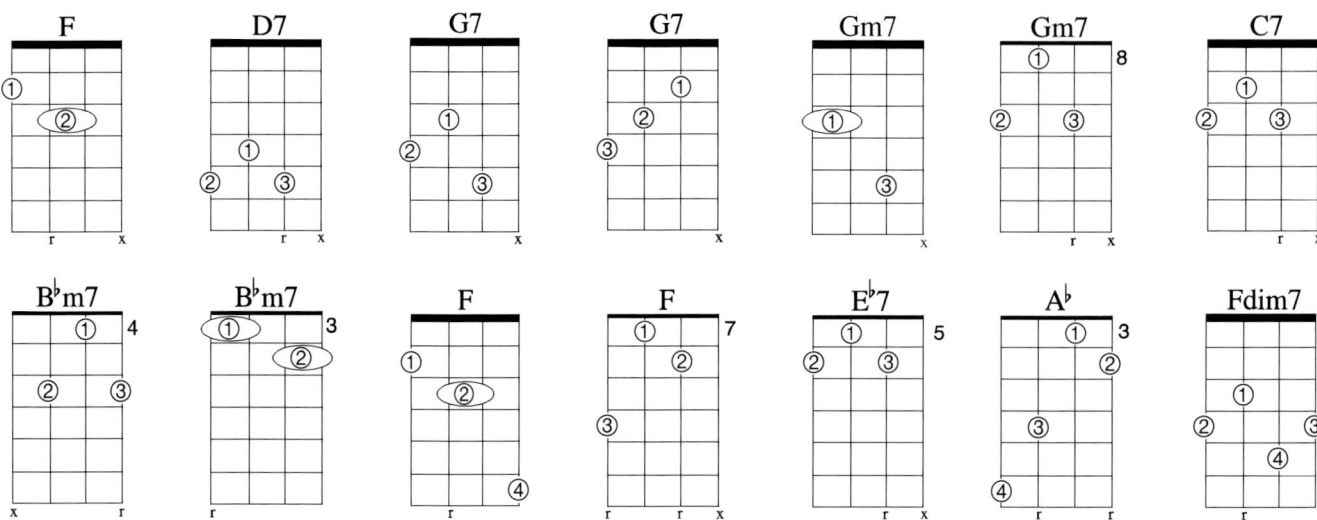

China Boy

Key of F, CD tracks 24-26
D. Winfree & P. Boutelje 1922

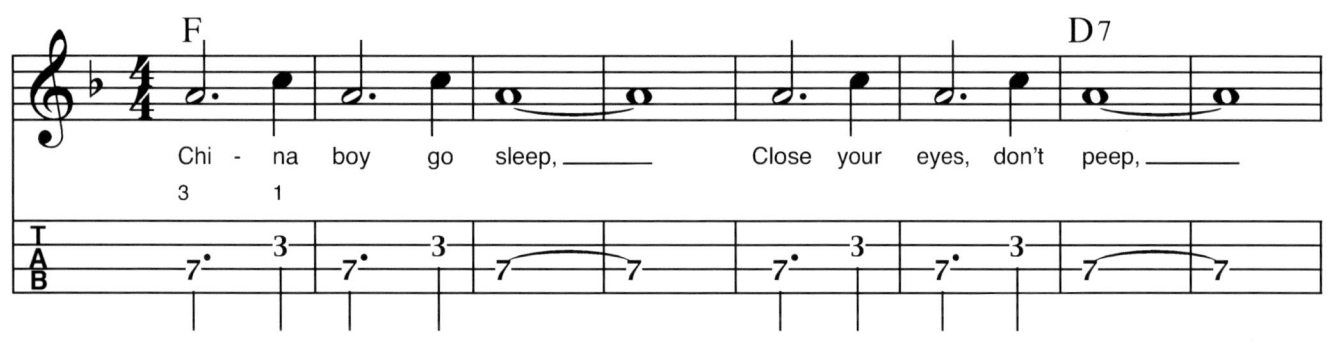
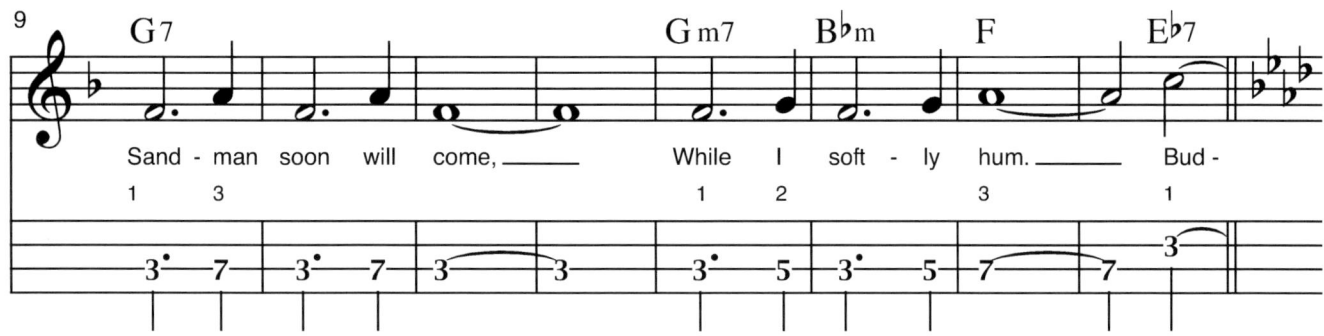
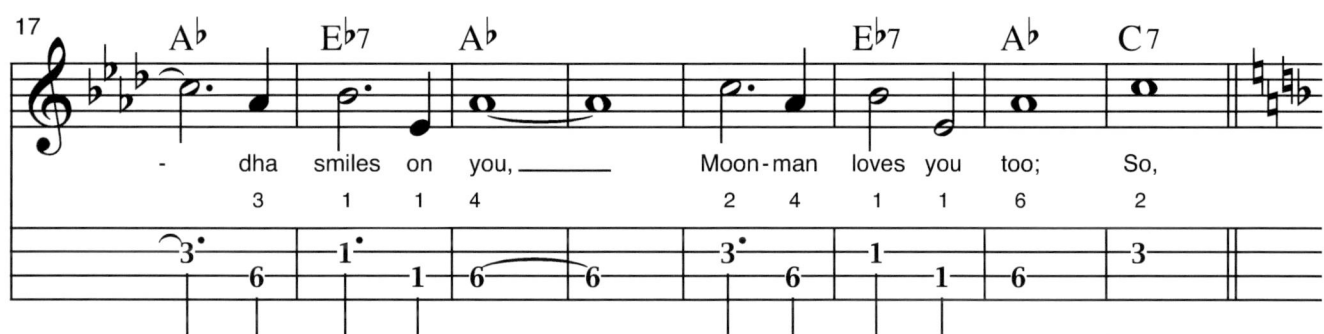
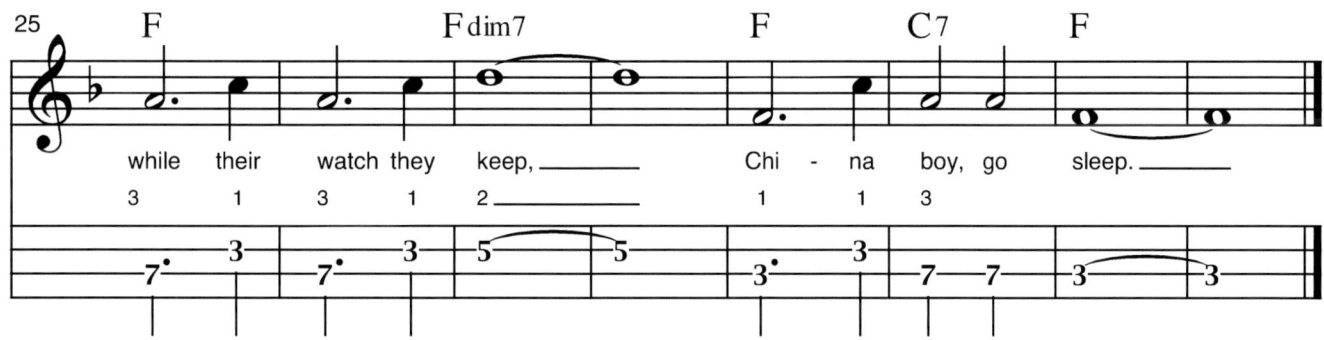

St. Louis Blues

"St. Louis Blues" was written by W.C. Handy in 1914 and was one of the first blues compositions to become a huge international hit. It's been a standard of jazz musicians all over the world for almost one hundred years and is still played everywhere. Handy also wrote "Memphis Blues," "Yellow Dog Blues," and "Beale Street Blues," among others.

Blues has been called the father of jazz and if you want to understand jazz you need to be familiar with the blues. The blues form is relatively simple and built on a twelve measure pattern: one measure of the I chord (in this case G), one of the IV (C), two of the I (G or G7), two of the IV (C or C7), two of the I, two of the V (D7), two of the I. Not every blues has these exact chords in this exact order. Often you'll encounter variations. One of the interesting things about "St. Louis Blues" is that it combines a blues progression with a sixteen measure bridge in a minor key played in a Latin rhythm. It's usually referred to as a tango but some people call it an *habanera*. This minor/Latin part is only played once, during the initial statement of the melody, sandwiched between two sets of major blues chord changes. The solos are played over the twelve bar major blues chord changes. There's more information on making your solos sound more "bluesy" on the next page.

The melody to "St. Louis Blues" can be played with a lot of open string notes on the mandolin. Play it first as written with open string notes then re-locate these open notes to fretted positions and play the melody there. It's important for you to learn all these melodies in closed position without open strings. You can download a closed position version of "St. Louis Blues" from my website: **www.musixnow.com**.

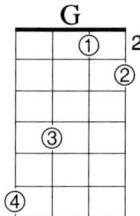
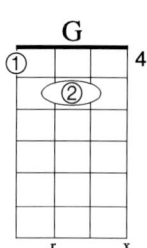
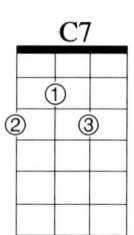
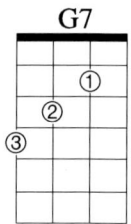
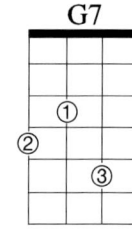

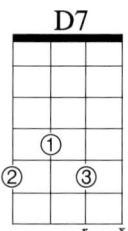
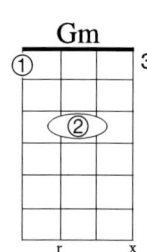
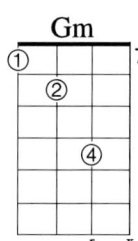
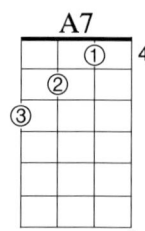

One of the keys to making your solos sound bluesy is to add "blue notes" to them. The blue notes I use most often are the flatted third and the flatted seventh tones of the scale. For "St. Louis Blues" in the key of G these blue notes would be Bb and F natural. The F# note is a scale tone. When we flat it we get F natural. See the scales below.

G major scale

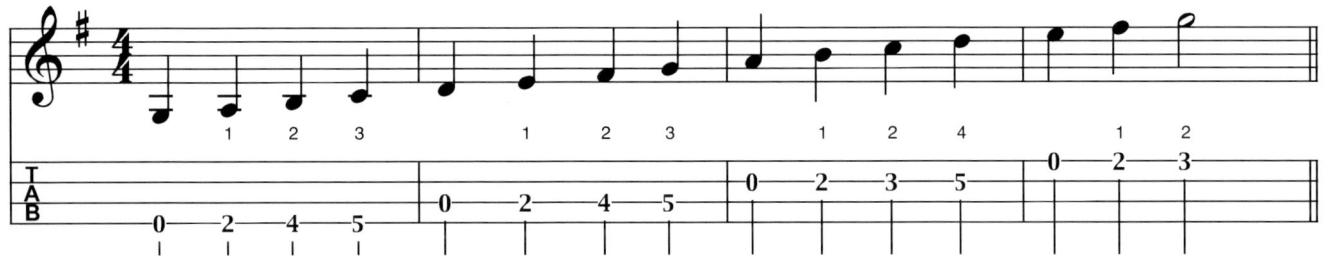

G major scale with blue notes: flatted third and seventh notes

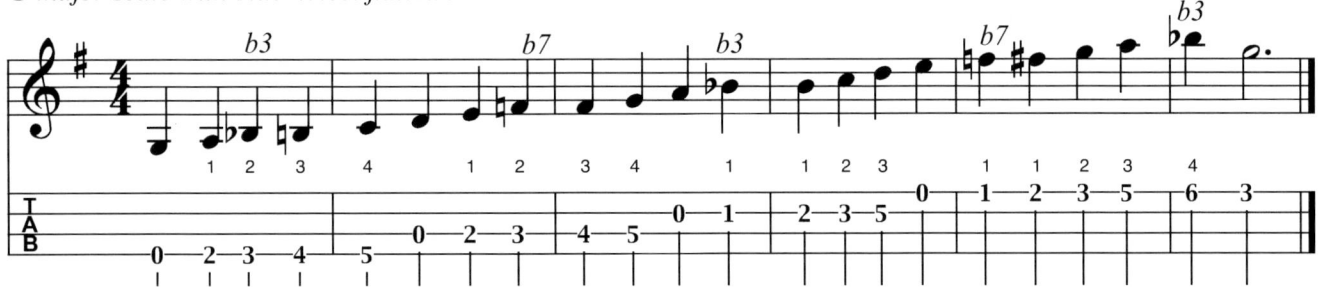

All music has a home tonality and a lot of the interest in a melody or solo comes from moving away and coming back to this tonality or "home." Blues notes provide tension as they work against the home tonality. Once you set up a tonality, your ear expects to hear the regular third and seventh tones. In the case of "St. Louis Blues" in the key of G major, those notes are B and F#. When you add the Bb and F natural notes, it's somewhat unexpected and interesting. Try adding the Bb and F natural tones to your solos. Make sure they reference the root of your home tone, in this case G, and resolve or come back to that tone.

The bridge in Gm is a whole different animal. Here you can use most of the notes of the G major scale with the flatted third and seventh tones, but you most certainly want to avoid or use very sparingly the notes B natural and F#. They're not part of the Gm scale. They would definitely add tension but not quite the right kind for blues. I suggest you stick to the Gm scale for soloing on the bridge.

G minor scale

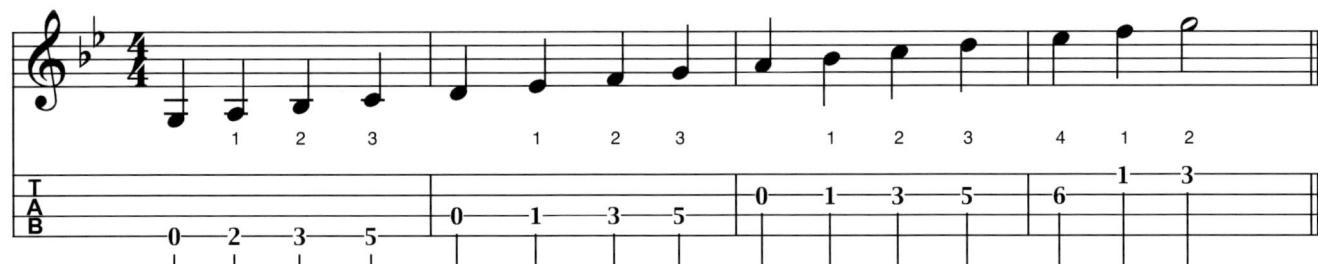

St. Louis Blues

Key of G, Gm, CD tracks 27-29
W.C. Handy, 1914

Arrangement © 2007 by Dix Bruce • www.musixnow.com

Rose Room

"Rose Room" dates back to 1914 and was a popular song that became an early jazz standard. Duke Ellington's "In a Mellow Tone" uses the same chord changes.

If you find the key of Ab difficult, it's probably because you haven't played in this key much. As I mentioned, it's important that you be able to play in all keys. The Quintette recorded "Rose Room" in the key of F but every band I've played with does it in Ab. Since we already have so many songs in F and nothing so far in Ab, I decided to arrange "Rose Room" in Ab. With a little bit of work, you, as a mandolinist, can transpose any song to any key. As you did with "China Boy," move the closed melody "down" one string so your first note is on the fourth string, first fret. You'll be in the key of Db. Once you've mastered that, move both positions up the fingerboard. Remember to relocate that lone open string note in measure thirteen to a closed position!

Jason Vanderford plays a simple four bar introduction that lands on the Eb7 or V chord of the key of Ab. You can clearly hear his comping style here — more rhythmic than harmonic — and he plays like this throughout the whole session. He reduces the sound of his chord to where it's barely more than a click. Like many of the Gypsy Swing players he uses a very thick pick that I'd guess is over an 1/8 inch thick. He's acting as a drummer and concentrating on the back beat. It is typical in Hot Club-style rhythm sections to have more than one rhythm player comping all the time. Django and Stephane usually had two rhythm guitarists in addition to Django. Listen to how beautifully they work together. With multiple rhythm players there can be a danger of actually diluting the groove if all the musicians aren't playing together. Everyone has to be playing the same type of rhythm at the same time and it helps for each player to pull back a bit and serve the band's groove and the soloist, not the ego. In these cases less is more. As you can hear, Jason is a wonderful player because he listens and plays to the groove.

In measures seven through ten the chord progression moves from Db to Dbm, or from IV ("four") to iv ("four minor"). Some players change to the Dbm in measure nine. In this version we change to the Dbm in measure ten. At the end of the first chorus, the band breaks on the first beat of the last two Ab measures. Again, I keep a rhythmic click going so we don't lose the groove. This type of break, prevalent in all styles of swing and jazz, gives the first soloist an extra two bars to launch into and set up the solo.

On the mandolin we have the choice of using tremolo to extend notes. To demonstrate I used tremolo on the slow recording of the melody but not on the fast so you can hear the differences.

I recently played a gig where the band performed "Rose Room" as a tango. Give it a try!

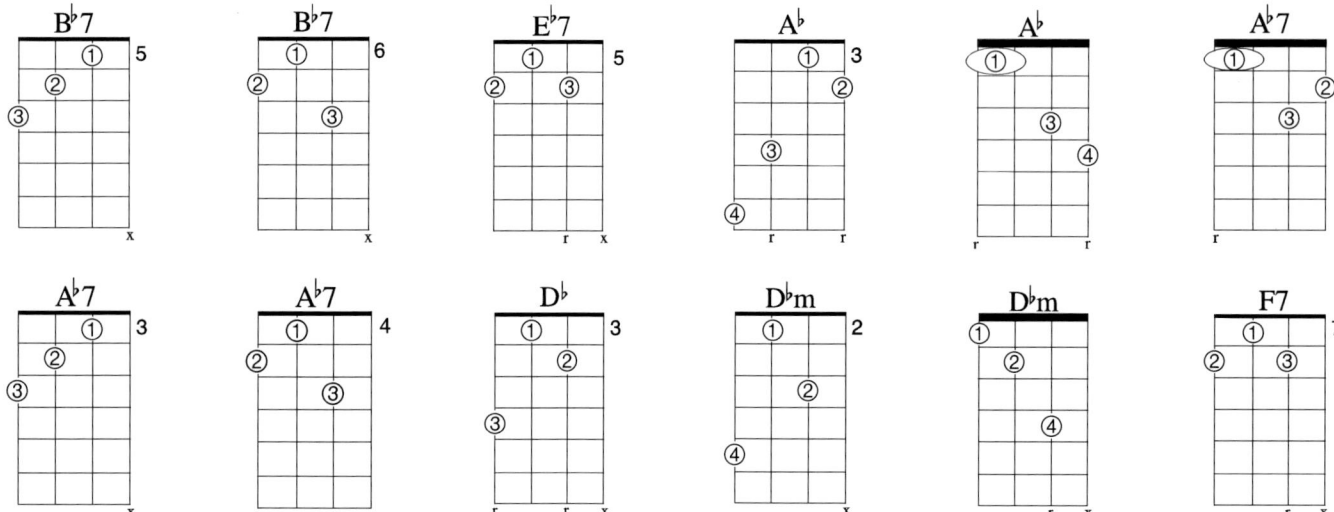

Rose Room

Key of Ab, CD tracks 30-32

A. Hickman & H. Williams, 1917

Dark Eyes

"Dark Eyes" is probably Russian in origin, certainly Eastern European, and it's one of those songs that evokes wagons around a campfire, dancing and singing late into the night in a gypsy camp. It's loaded with potential for emotion and passion. Our version begins in 3/4 (page 35) and moves into 4/4 (page 36) with a six measure transition. The transition begins with four measures of solo guitar chords, shown below with mandolin chords and tablature, to set up the new meter and tempo. Try playing it on the mandolin. The transition is followed with a two measure solo bass fill by Steve Hanson. Solos can be played over either meter, but they're usually played over the 4/4 section, as we've done here. The lyrics are transliterated from the Russian.

Transition chords:

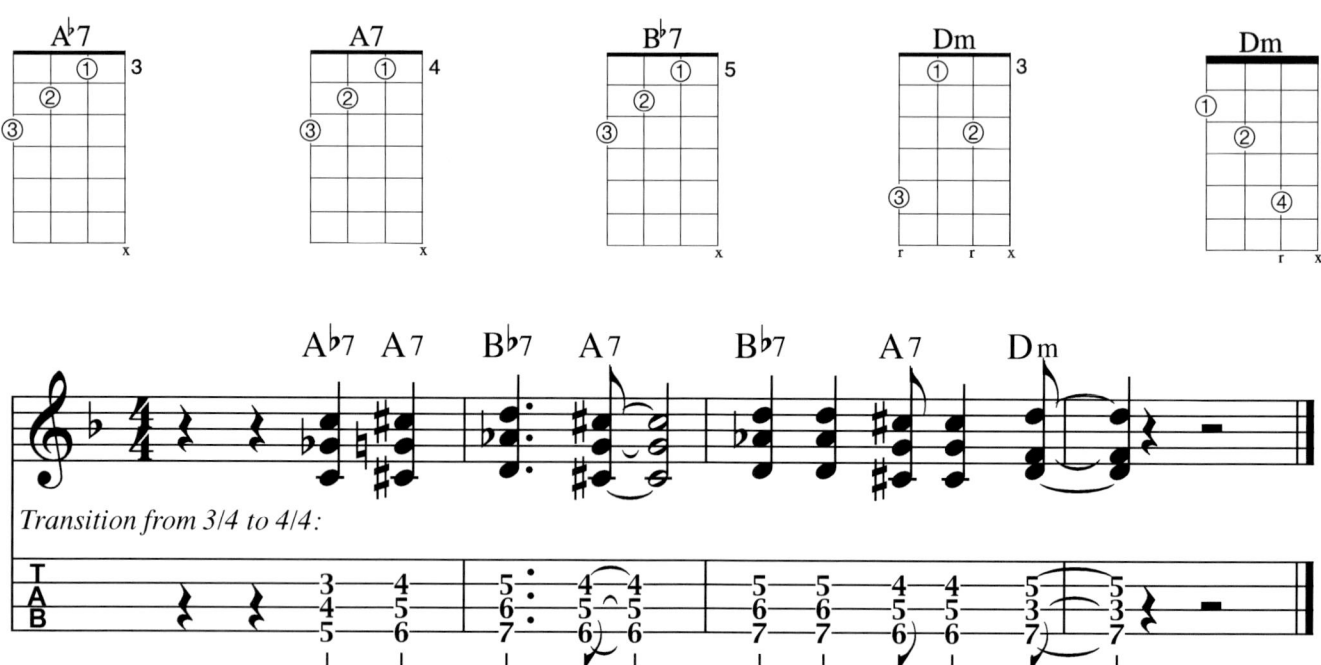

The ending to "Dark Eyes" has a repeat of the final four measures with a *ritard* or slow down on the repeat. If you decide to use this type of ending be sure to warn your fellow players to expect such a thing. If you're the band leader, give clues that something unexpected is about to happen and lead the change in rhythm.

"Dark Eyes" chords:

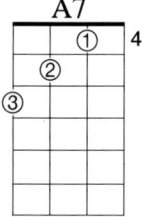 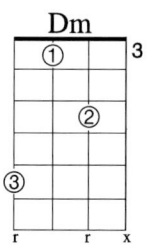 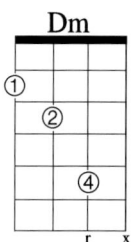 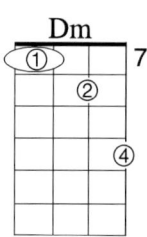 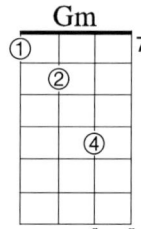

Dark Eyes

Key of Dm, 3/4 time, CD tracks 33-35

Traditional, Russian

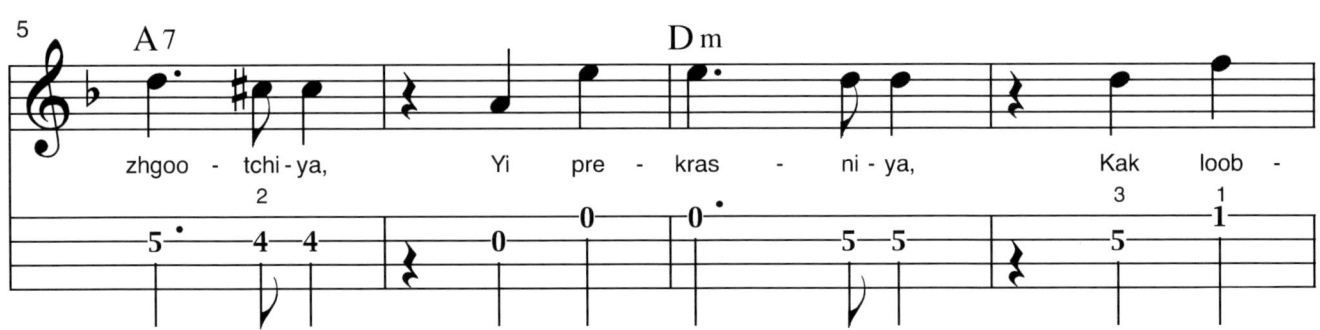

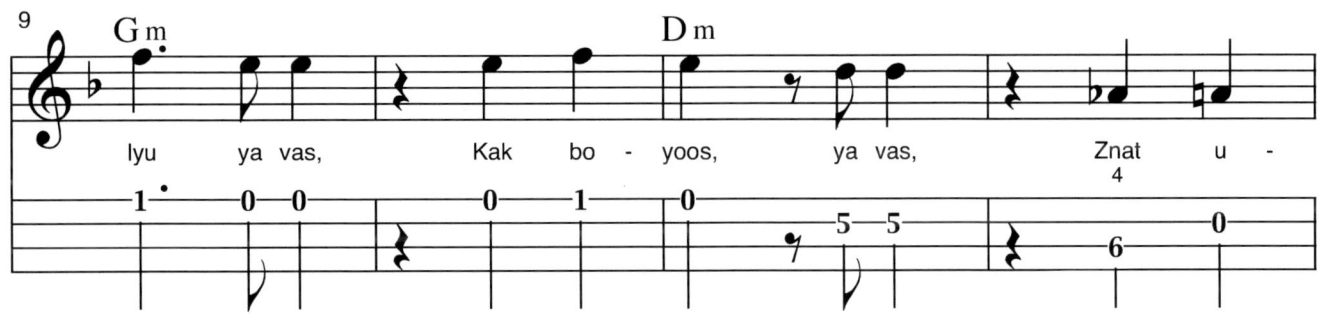

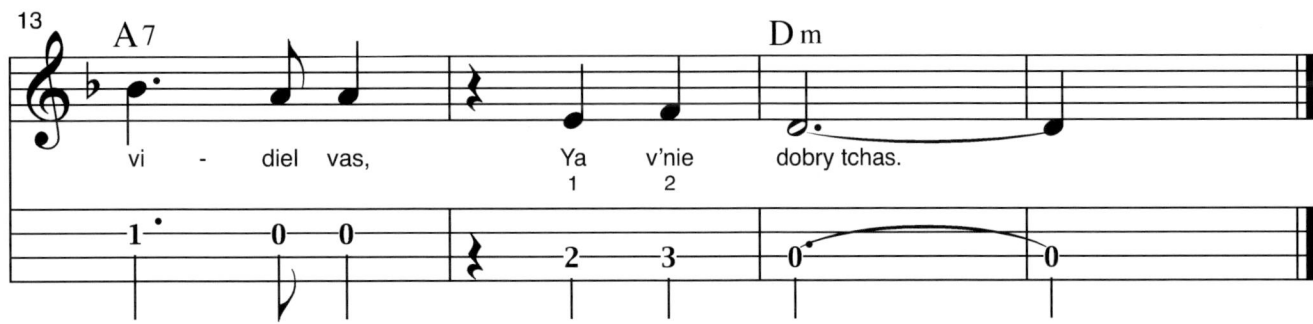

Arrangement © 2007 by Dix Bruce • www.musixnow.com

Dark Eyes

Key of Dm, 4/4 time, CD tracks 33-35

Traditional, Russian

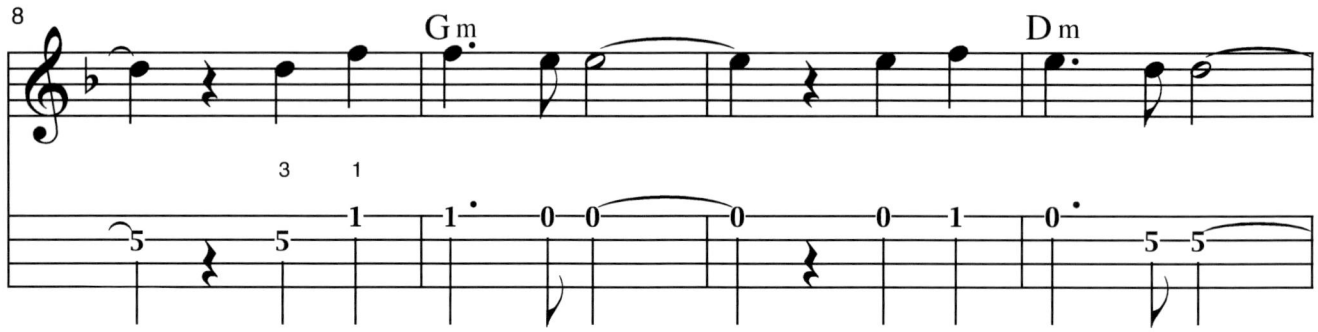

Last time repeat last 4 bars twice, ritard last repeat.

Arrangement © 2007 by Dix Bruce • www.musixnow.com

Swingin' Like '42

"Swingin' Like '42" is based on a popular Reinhardt and Grappelli composition called "Swing 42." They also recorded different tunes titled "Swing 39," "Swing 41," and "Swing 48." Generically speaking, "Swingin' Like '42" has what are called "rhythm changes." These are chord changes based on the 1930 George and Ira Gershwin song "I Got Rhythm" and literally thousands of other songs have these same changes. The classic chord changes are I ("one" C), vi ("six" Am), ii ("two" Dm), V ("five" G7), over and over again. Next to blues changes, "rhythm" changes are probably the second most popular in jazz. Musicians often identify a song as "rhythm changes in C" or "rhythm changes in Ab." "Swingin' Like '42," which is in the key of C, has some additional changes and substitutions (minor seven chords for the regular minor chords) but the basic is still considered "rhythm changes" or variations of I vi ii V. "Swingin' Like '42" modulates from the key of C to the key of E and back and uses the same progression I ("one" E), vi ("six" C#m), ii ("two" F#m), V ("five" B7) in the key of E.

In the mid-1970s mandolinist and "dawg" music creator David Grisman often played "Swing 42" in his early Quintets. This popularized the tune among acoustic string jazz and bluegrass players and it became a kind of standard in those genres. The melody to "Swingin' Like '42" will work as a solo on the changes to "Swing '42."

I use the open fourth string G several times in the melody to "Swingin' Like '42" so it makes sense to me to use other open string notes too. I love the timber of that open fourth string on my Schneider mandolin. Since the lowest note in the melody is the lowest note on the mandolin, you can't transpose it to a lower key. Try transposing it up in pitch to other keys. I played a variation in measure seven on the up-to-speed recording. Can you figure it out?

If you play "Swingin' Like '42" more than once through, use the chord changes from the first ending for the last two measures. These changes (C, C#dim7, Dm7, G7) will bring you back to the top of the form. Use the changes as written in the last two measures when you end the song the last time.

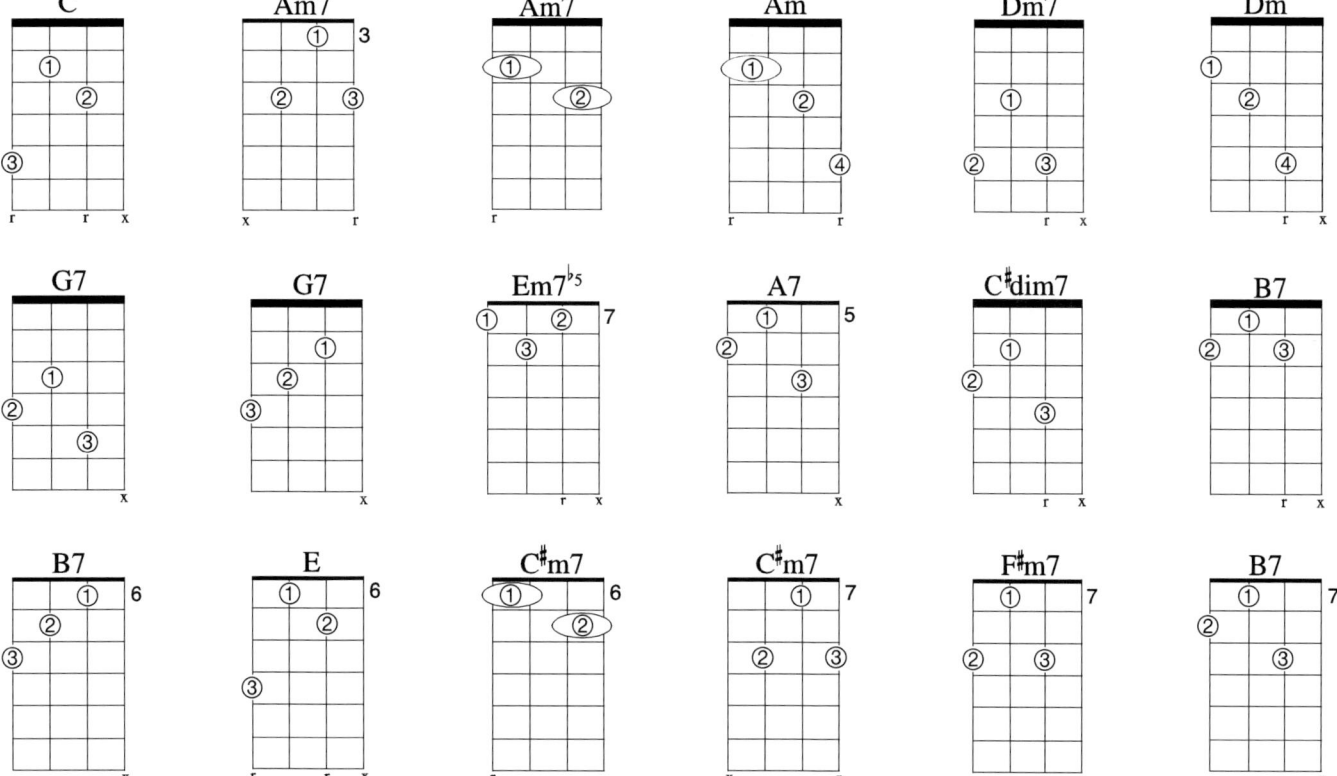

Swingin' Like '42

Key of C, CD tracks 36-38 *Dix Bruce, 2007*

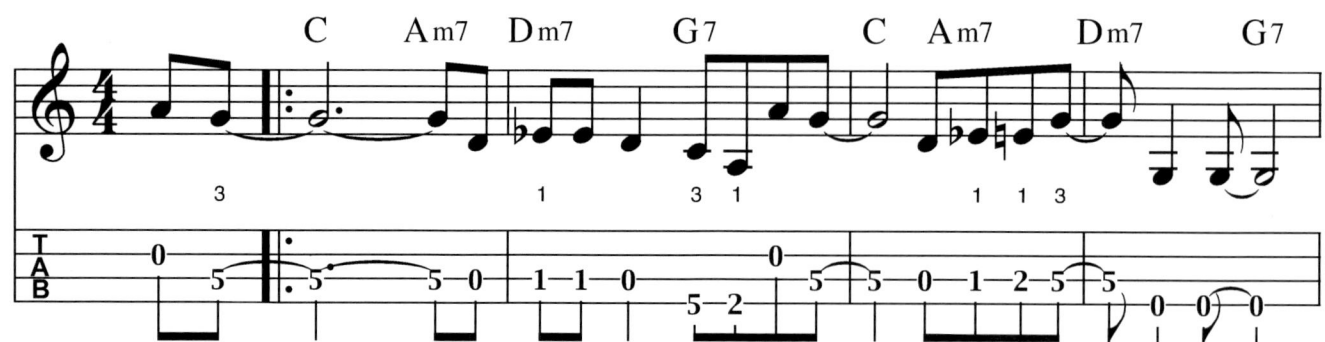

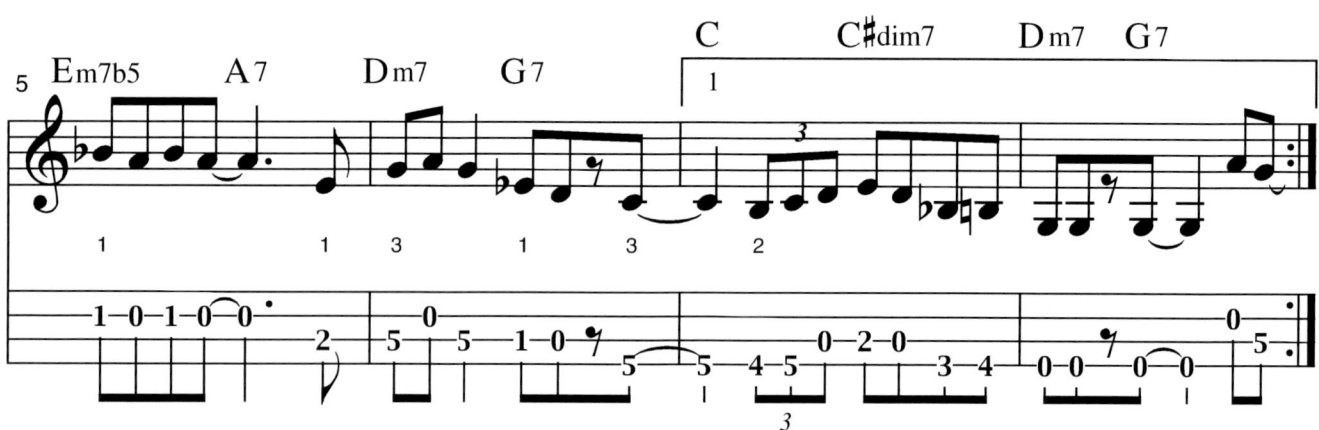

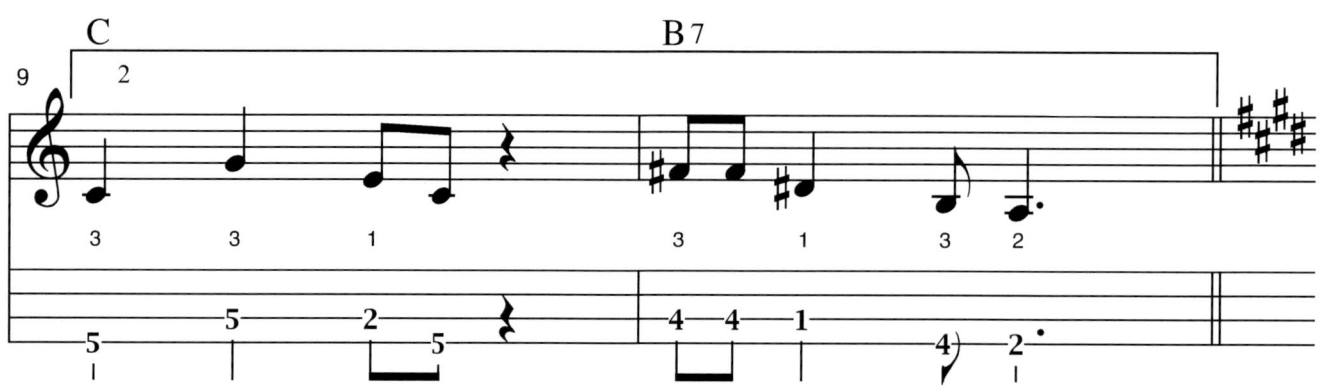

Copyright © 2007 by Dix Bruce • Dix Bruce Music (BMI) • www.musixnow.com

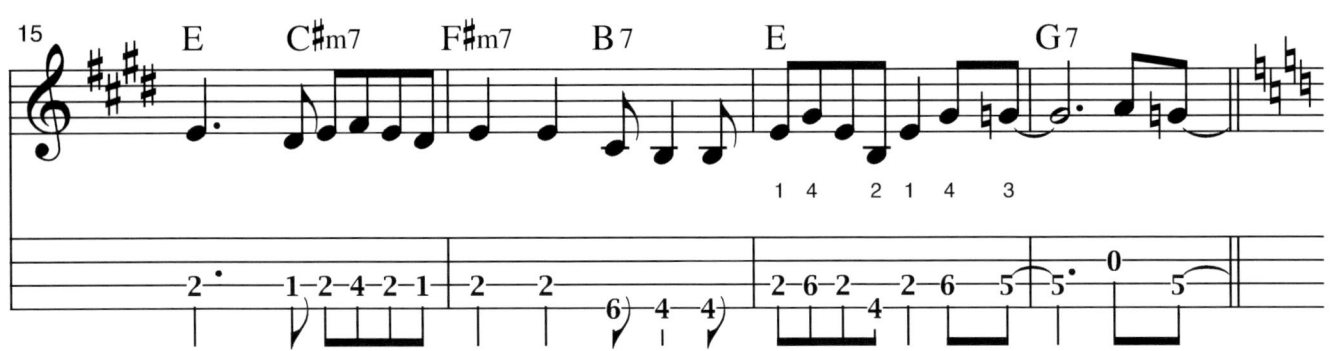
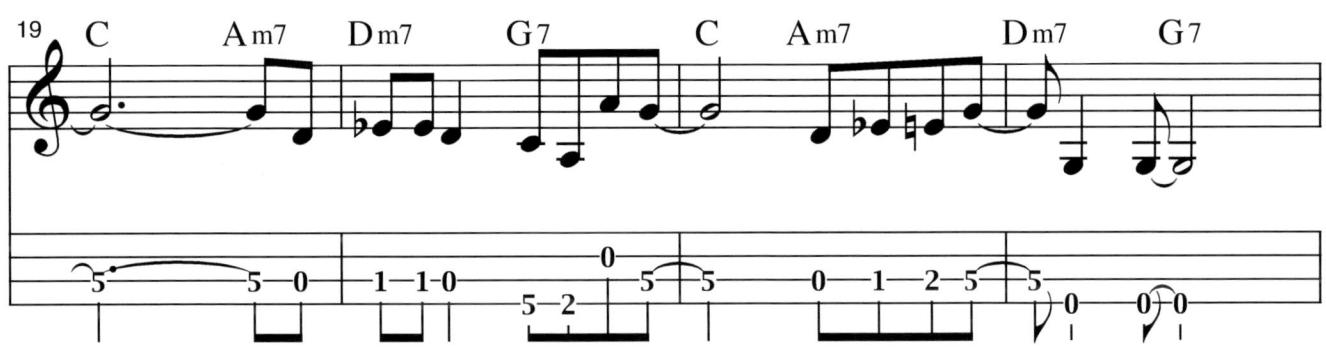
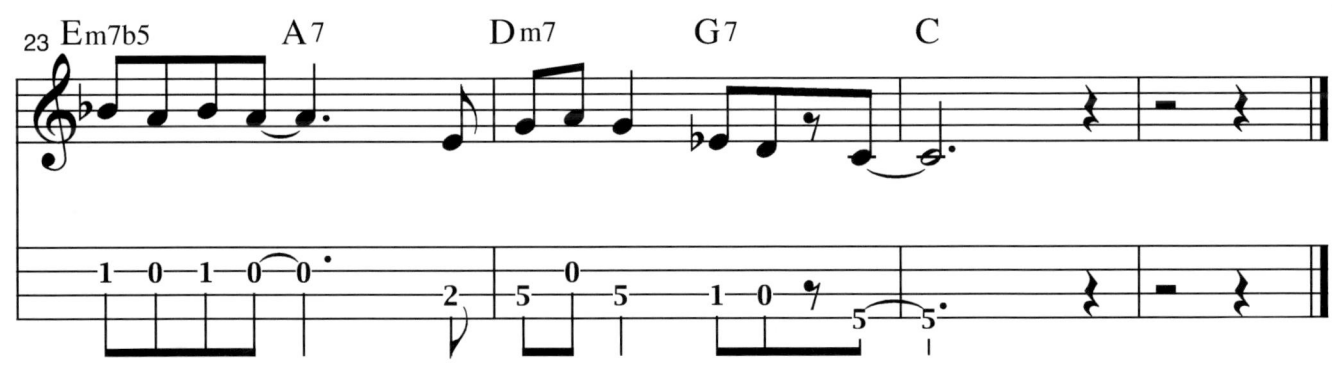

CD Contents

1. Tuning *(1:02)*
2. The Gypsy Swing rhythm comp *(2:04)*
3. Avalon melody slow *(1:14)*
4. Avalon melody up-to-speed *(:39)*
5. Avalon band track *(3:37)*
6. The Sheik of Araby melody slow *(1:17)*
7. The Sheik of Araby melody up-to-speed *(:43)*
8. The Sheik of Araby track *(3:06)*
9. Some of These Days melody slow *(1:33)*
10. Some of These Days melody up-to-speed *(:49)*
11. Some of These Days track *(3:36)*
12. After You've Gone melody slow *(1:21)*
13. After You've Gone melody up-to-speed *(:44)*
14. After You've Gone track *(3:17)*
15. Baby Won't You Please Come Home? melody slow *(1:16)*
16. Baby Won't You Please Come Home? melody up-to-speed *(:43)*
17. Baby Won't You Please Come Home? track *(4:15)*
18. Swing in Minor melody slow *(1:17)*
19. Swing in Minor melody up-to-speed *(:50)*
20. Swing in Minor track *(3:04)*
21. Chicago melody slow *(1:20)*
22. Chicago melody up-to-speed *(:47)*
23. Chicago track *(4:08)*
24. China Boy melody slow *(:57)*
25. China Boy melody up-to-speed *(:37)*
26. China Boy track *(3:34)*
27. St. Louis Blues melody slow *(2:58)*
28. St. Louis Blues melody up-to-speed *(1:50)*
29. St. Louis Blues track *(3:29)*
30. Rose Room melody slow *(1:27)*
31. Rose Room melody up-to-speed *(:51)*
32. Rose Room track *(4:11)*
33. Dark Eyes melody slow *(1:30)*
34. Dark Eyes melody up-to-speed *(:52)*
35. Dark Eyes track *(3:57)*
36. Swingin' Like '42 melody slow *(1:27)*
37. Swingin' Like '42 melody up-to-speed *(:47)*
38. Swingin' Like '42 track *(4:04)*

Index

A

After You've Gone 16
Avalon 8

B

Baby Won't You Please Come Home? 18

C

CD Contents 40
Chicago 23
China Boy 26
Contents 2

D

Dark Eyes 34

H

How to Work with the Book and CD 5

I

Introduction to Gypsy Swing 3

R

Rose Room 32

S

Sheik of Araby, The 10
Some of These Days 13
St. Louis Blues 28
Swing Mandolin Rhythm 7
Swingin' Like 42 37
Swing in Minor 20

Swing & Jazz Mandolin: Chords & Rhythm DVD by Dix Bruce. Moveable chords, comping, chord numbering, transposing, 8 great Swing & Jazz songs. Play-along format. Teaches everything you need to know to get up and swinging on the mandolin! **www.musixnow.com**